PRAISE FOR *YOUR LIFE IS GOD'S STORY*

Tim Dilena's latest book reads like he preaches. Tim's words are clear, simple, gripping, and convicting. Those who apply the teaching in this book will find that their life will change for the better. Some of us who are preachers are not so good at writing; some great writers are not so good at communicating. Tim has the rare gift of being equally good at both preaching and writing.

R. T. Kendall, minister, Westminster
Chapel, London (1977–2022)

Many of us struggle with the way the story of our lives is going to play out. This accessible book, rich in insight into God, the Bible, and our contemporary world, is an encouragement to a deeper, richer, and more confident faith.

J John, evangelist

Tim Dilena delivers God's Word every week and pastors one of the greatest churches in the world. His is a voice that needs to be heard. And that's why I'm so glad he has written *Your Life Is God's Story*. You will discover how to live God's purpose for your life as this gifted, experienced pastor opens God's Word in a clear, Christ-centered way.

Jack Graham, senior pastor, Prestonwood Baptist Church

As a fourteen-year National Hockey League veteran, I learned a thing or two about fighting. You begin by grabbing hold and then wait for your opportunity to connect. Pastor Tim is a master at grabbing hold of his readers, captivating them through story and then connecting with deep biblical truth that sticks. I've always been a fan of the way Tim Dilena communicates. After reading this book, you will b...

...m Burt, former NHL player

Tim Dilena has a biblical perspective on how God's story for our lives often unfolds. It doesn't always look the way we want it to look. But it is still God's way. If your way seems messy and hard today, you may find the answer to why in these pages. The Bible promises in Romans 8:28 that in whatever God sends our way, He is always working for our good.

Carter Conlon, general overseer, Times Square Church, Inc.

Tim Dilena lives and writes with a pastor's heart. His love for people and his love for the Bible sing out from every page of this book. Let Pastor Tim give you a set of night vision goggles to see God's way in this dark world.

Hance Dilbeck, president and CEO,
GuideStone Financial Resources

Tim Dilena offers a rare and wonderful treasure, letting you in on insights that have been undiscovered by so many who need infusions of hope and courage. This book tells of real lives in Scripture, revival history, and contemporary culture. And it also tells of *your* life and *your* story—which is God's story.

William (Winkie) Pratney, author and youth evangelist

In this pastoral, powerful, and inspirational Bible-based book, Tim Dilena reaches back to the biblical world, takes its characters by the hand, and leads them into our world. This book is not just a window through which you see past lives; it is a lens through which you see your own life mapped over these lives. If you are discouraged, you will find encouragement. If you are plagued with failure, you will be healed. If you have lost your compass, this book will show you true spiritual north. The energetic, warm, and winsome pastor that is Tim Dilena infuses this book with heartfelt compassion.

Joel C. Gregory, George W. Truett endowed professor
of preaching, Baylor University's Truett Seminary

Pastor Tim Dilena beautifully lays out the ways God works through the mountaintop moments and the valleys of despair in our lives. Knowing that God guides our path gives us the confidence to keep moving forward. Tim's book is a must-read for any believer seeking God's will at any stage of life.

Dr. Adam C. Wright, president, Dallas Baptist University

None of us escape pain and sorrow in our lifetime. We all need a strong word of encouragement. Pastor Tim Dilena delivers a timely message that I know will lift you up to new heights no matter what you're facing now.

Gary Wilkerson, president, World Challenge

Tim Dilena is a man of God whom I honor and respect greatly. His love for God and God's people is contagious. I know this book can change your life forever because trusting God's plan with your whole life allows you to experience God's best your whole life long!

Cece Winans, award-winning gospel singer

There are delicate blank spaces in our lives that leave us unsure and confused. The writings of Pastor Dilena reinforce God's power in those times, while allowing us to see His glory in the end where victory is achieved. This book is a must-read.

Yvette Hamilton, WNBA chaplain

Your Life is God's Story is filled with true stories that will hold your attention and engaging teachings that apply God's truth to today's pain. Tim Dilena writes like a soul whose faith is anchored in the Word and is lived out in a real world. His style is relatable, his source is scriptural, and his practical applications to our lives can strengthen us to walk this journey with integrity in troubled times.

Alicia Britt Chole, author of *The Night Is Normal: A Guide Through Spiritual Pain*

Rarely has there been a time when we've needed a biblically based message of hope and encouragement more than we do now. Pastor Tim Dilena delivers this message, urging us to cling to God and His Word so we can weather the storms we are facing and those we will continue to face.

Nicky Cruz, author, evangelist

YOUR LIFE IS GOD'S STORY

YOUR LIFE IS GOD'S STORY

TRUSTING GOD'S
PLAN THROUGH LIFE'S
UPS AND DOWNS

TIM DILENA

ZONDERVAN REFLECTIVE

Your Life Is God's Story
Copyright © 2024 by Tim Dilena

Published in Grand Rapids, Michigan, by Zondervan. Zondervan is a registered trademark of The Zondervan Corporation, L.L.C., a wholly owned subsidiary of HarperCollins Christian Publishing, Inc.

Requests for information should be addressed to customercare@harpercollins.com.

Zondervan titles may be purchased in bulk for educational, business, fundraising, or sales promotional use. For information, please email SpecialMarkets@Zondervan.com.

ISBN 978-0-310-15585-0 (audio)

Library of Congress Cataloging-in-Publication Data

Names: Dilena, Timothy, 1963- author.
Title: Your life is God's story : trusting God's plan through life's ups and downs / Timothy Dilena.
Description: Grand Rapids, Michigan : Zondervan Reflective, [2024]
Identifiers: LCCN 2023044818 (print) | LCCN 2023044819 (ebook) | ISBN 9780310155829 (softcover) | ISBN 9780310155836 (ebook)
Subjects: LCSH: Trust in God—Christianity. | Faith—Religious aspects Christianity. | BISAC: RELIGION / Christian Living / Spiritual Growth | RELIGION / Biblical Studies / General
Classification: LCC BV4637 .D445 2024 (print) | LCC BV4637 (ebook) | DDC 234/.23—dc23/eng/20240124
LC record available at https://lccn.loc.gov/2023044818
LC ebook record available at https://lccn.loc.gov/2023044819

Cover design: Bruce Gore | Gore Studio, Inc.
Cover image: © Hecke61 / Shutterstock
Interior design: Sara Colley

Printed in the United States of America

24 25 26 27 28 LBC 5 4 3 2 1

To my friend and mentor Dr. R. T. Kendall—
the two words I use
to end each email to you
sum up how I feel
about your impact on my life:
"Your Timothy"

CONTENTS

FOREWORD

I remember it as if it were just yesterday. I was a young teenaged convert to the faith when someone handed me a book titled *The Cross and the Switchblade* by David Wilkerson. Like many young believers in my generation, I had a fire lit in my heart for evangelism that still burns brightly today more than fifty years later. As the years unfolded, it became my great joy to get to know David and to love him. During my days of pastoring in Fort Lauderdale, he would join us for "spring break" and preach the gospel to the thousands of college students who flooded our beaches every spring.

Now in my later years of ministry, there walks a young man into my life by the name of Tim Dilena, himself a product of the ministry of David Wilkerson and now pastor of the church he founded. To know Tim is to love him and to respect him. Just a few moments in his presence will lighten your load and brighten your road. He is, hands down, the real deal.

It has been my privilege on many occasions recently to

preach in his pulpit at Times Square Church in New York City. As Tim reveals in this book, there is the "power of story." This is never more obvious than in the life of Tim Dilena. He has emerged as one of the great young pastor-evangelists of the Western world and beyond. From his platform in Times Square he challenges thousands of people from multiple nations every week inside one of the most beautiful worship buildings in all the world. Add to this the weekly outreach to multitudes of people in scores of countries who are touched with the gospel through Times Square's weekly online outreach, and you have a pastor and people who are making a difference in their own "Jerusalem" and all the way to the ends of the earth for Jesus' sake.

I predict this volume you now hold in your hand will be only the first of many that will flow from his prolific pen. Get ready. We are going to hear a lot about the Christ who is alive in the life of Tim Dilena in the years to come. This is his story. And when you get caught up in the flow of these pages, it will become your story as well. Read it and reap!

After all, your story is God's story!

O. S. HAWKINS, PhD, chancellor, Southwestern Baptist Theological Seminary, author of the bestselling "Code Series," including *The Joshua Code*

FOUR WORDS THAT CHANGED MY LIFE

One evening in 1958, David Wilkerson saw a copy of a *LIFE* magazine that featured several New York City gang members on the cover. He looked at the faces of the teens who were on trial for the brutal murder of a paraplegic teen in Central Park. As Wilkerson prayed for those boys, he sensed that God wanted him to leave the comforts of his country church and go preach to the gangs of NYC. Answering the call, he decided he was going to preach on the streets of Brooklyn, the epicenter of gang activity.

One day, the skinny preacher stood up on a park bench and began to speak the life-giving words of Jesus to every passerby. Two police officers stood on that Brooklyn street corner that day. One of them was growing visibly uncomfortable. "What seems to be the problem?" the second policeman asked. The first policeman explained that he was worried and didn't think Reverend Wilkerson should preach on that corner because of the gang problems in the area. The second officer surveyed the scene, and then he uttered these four words: *"Let the man preach."*

God came to New York City in a special way that day. As David Wilkerson preached, Nicky Cruz, the warlord of the worst gang in New York, listened. As a result, Cruz and hundreds of gang members came to Christ.[1] The most successful drug rehab program in the world, Teen Challenge, was launched. Nicky Cruz would go on to become one of the era's most effective evangelists.[2] And God would give birth to one of the most vibrant churches in the world, Times Square Church. Thousands of people from 120 countries came together in one of Broadway's largest theaters to bring the gospel to New York City and to the world.

■　■　■

Let the man preach.

The police officer who spoke those words more than fifty-five years ago was my father, Paul Dilena. Through God's miraculous orchestration, I now preach from the pulpit at Times Square Church. Christian author Philip Yancey wrote, "I have learned that faith means trusting in advance what will only make sense in reverse."[3] As I look back on those events, I can see God's fingerprints all over them. What God was orchestrating when my Italian immigrant father crossed paths with that Pennsylvanian minister could never have been scripted by human hands.

At times, life can seem like a bunch of random experiences and places. But just wait! In the end, we'll see that it's all part of God's elaborate plan to prepare us for a greater purpose and destiny. God is orchestrating thousands of seemingly random events for an amazing future. We just need to trust the process.

We all need a new set of lenses to see experiences and events in a different way. This book is going to be your night vision goggles, enabling you to see God's bigger plan when you feel like he has left you in the dark. This book is going to help you see God's purposes more clearly in both catastrophic experiences and daily, mundane events. It will help you see God's fingerprints on each day of your life.

I want you to take a journey into the lives of people whom God used greatly. If you don't know the end of their story, remember this: trust the process! Everything comes together in the end. Some of these stories will sound familiar, and you may well be able to put your name in their plots. My desire is that when you see how God gets people to their intended destinies, you will have a renewed passion to not only endure but also realize it all comes together in the end. So get ready. I believe you will be saying as you read on, "Been there, done that." You will also have some revealing moments as you read and realize, "So this is what I am going through," and maybe even, "This is why I am going through this." For many, these stories won't be just words on a page, but rather mirrors and even answers to your journey. When we know God is working behind the scenes, we get a new perspective that brings a new strength because, in the end, the story will all make sense.

THE POWER OF STORIES

Your Life Is God's Story tells God-stories that testify to God's involvement in people's lives. It contains eleven stories from the lives of Bible characters—stories that will inform, inflame, and inspire. It will help you see God's perfect process in people's lives. It will inspire you to go back and reread their stories. And I know that it will give you content to light a fire in the hearts and souls of the next generation.

The apostle Paul reminded the Roman believers, "Everything that was written in the past was written to teach us, so that through the endurance taught in the Scriptures and the encouragement they provide we might have hope" (Romans 15:4 NIV). The biblical stories you'll read in this book aren't just stories—they're *your* stories. They were written for you. *Your Life Is God's Story* is an inspirational tool to help you mine the gold in these stories found in God's Word.

You will find stories of betrayal, false accusations, and survival. You will find stories of people saying no to sexual immorality and yes to moral purity. There are stories of politicians who became amazing witnesses under very difficult circumstances. You will find stories of kids from dysfunctional homes who rose to success.

As you read the stories of these eleven lives and see the hand of God on their journey, spread their stories to others. Tell people, "I understand what happened to David because it happened to me." *Your Life Is God's Story* will give you language to tell these stories to the next generation. I've included discussion questions at the end of each chapter to help spark conversations.

Someone once said, "History is really His-story." It's God's story. It's the story of God's activity in people's lives. It's seeing God on every page of your past, present, and future days as you live out the remainder of your time on this earth.

CHAPTER 1

SHARING SCAR STORIES WITH HEZEKIAH

It is doubtful whether God can bless a man
greatly until He has hurt him deeply.
A. W. Tozer, *The Root of the Righteous*

I have scars on my body, and each of them tells a unique story about a particular day in my life. Some tell stories of my own negligence, and some tell stories about the people around me acting irresponsibly. They relate a bit of my life —my story—to others.

My friend Kevin Ramsby has literally six feet of scars on his body. Now, that's a lot of scars! On August 10, 2008, at 3:00 a.m., Kevin was startled out of his sleep by a crashing noise. Someone had broken into his home. Without hesitation, he grabbed a tennis racket and began yelling, hoping to scare off the intruder, and then raced down the steps to the first floor. Kevin didn't know that the intruder, Wesley, was racing up that same staircase, wielding a scar maker—the largest knife from Kevin's kitchen.

They collided. Wesley lunged with his knife and ripped Kevin's stomach open. He then proceeded to stab him in the neck and back. At one point, Kevin tried to grab the knife to stop the stabbing, only for the knife to cut through the tendons of his fingers. Wesley stabbed Kevin so many times that eventually Kevin fell to the ground in a pool of his own blood.

What happened next is nothing short of a miracle. While he was lying in his own blood, bleeding out, alone but for the crazed man searching his home for valuables that he could pawn for crack money, Kevin sensed that his life was coming to an end. He began to pray for his family. He uttered a prayer that only a father could pray: "Lord, don't let my children be bitter with you and come to hate the ministry."

Out of nowhere, he heard the voice of God say to him, *They still need you.*

At that, Kevin found a supernatural strength to get up. Holding his intestines in place, he made his way out the side door of his home to his neighbor's house.

When the ambulance and the police arrived, they found a man covered in so much blood that they couldn't tell his ethnicity. While the ambulance rushed Kevin to Detroit's Henry Ford Hospital, the police went inside Kevin's house to find the assailant. When they saw the pool of blood on the floor where Kevin had been lying, they were astounded by how much blood he had lost. What shocked them most, however, was that they saw *no* bloody footprints leading from Kevin's house to the neighbor's. It seemed impossible—or were they perhaps witnessing a miracle?[1]

I firmly *believe* Kevin is a living miracle. Kevin was held in the palms of God's hands that night.

He suffered from thirty-seven stab wounds, but doctors determined that not one of those stab wounds touched a vital organ in Kevin's body. A few weeks later, that hero of the faith walked out of the hospital alive but bearing six feet of scars.

There will always be scars, but there will always be miracles as well. We miss the miracles when we focus on the scars.

The Bible tells a story of scars on both the inside and outside that took place thousands of years before Kevin's tragic night. It's a scar story about what parents can do to their children. The main character is Hezekiah, who was considered one of two good kings to rule the southern kingdom of Judah.

When pain is part of God's process in our lives, those experiences have the ability to do something a book or a classroom falls short in being able to accomplish. They go deep. Solomon says in Proverbs 20:30, "Bruising wounds clean away evil, and blows cleanse the innermost parts." Where information reaches the head, scars can go to the innermost parts and teach lessons never to be forgotten. Something deeply profound happened to Kevin, and something deeply profound took place in Hezekiah.

ANOTHER SCAR STORY

During the reign of Solomon's son Rehoboam, the kingdom of Israel divided into two nations: the northern kingdom of Israel and the southern kingdom of Judah. In the books of Kings and Chronicles, we find that none of the nineteen kings of the northern kingdom of Israel receive a positive assessment, and only two of the twenty kings of Judah receive a positive assessment—Josiah and Hezekiah.

Hezekiah's scars are part of his journey to the throne and to revival. His story begins in 2 Kings 18:

> Now it came about in the third year of Hoshea, the son of Elah king of Israel, that Hezekiah the son of Ahaz king of Judah became king. He was twenty-five years old when he became king, and he reigned for twenty-nine years in Jerusalem; and his mother's name was Abi the daughter of Zechariah. He did what was right in the sight of the LORD, in accordance with everything that his father David had done. He removed the high places and smashed the memorial stones to pieces, and cut down the Asherah. He also crushed to pieces the bronze serpent that Moses had made, for until those days the sons

of Israel had been burning incense to it; and it was called Nehushtan. He trusted in the LORD, the God of Israel; and after him there was no one like him among all the kings of Judah, nor among those who came before him. (2 Kings 18:1–5)

When I read this description of Hezekiah, I found myself thinking about Hezekiah's father. As a parent, I was eager to learn how this young man had been raised to become one of the Old Testament's greatest kings. Now, we've all heard the phrase, "The apple doesn't fall far from the tree." In this case, the apple was Hezekiah, and the tree was Ahaz.

One of the ways my wife, Cindy, and I invest in our children to guide them to becoming like a Josiah or a Hezekiah is by praying with them and for them every night. We felt like God gave us certain prayers to pray over them each night. They have heard these words ever since they were born. This is what we would pray over them for many years before bed: *God, protect their virginity; God, protect them physically; God, protect their destiny.*

A LESSON IN PARENTING?

Reading about young Hezekiah fulfilling his destiny intrigued me as a parent. I was eager to learn more about Ahaz, and I was certain his story would give me the key for successfully raising my kids to fulfill their destinies. So I began flipping through my Bible to learn more about Ahaz. Here's how we're introduced to him:

> In the seventeenth year of Pekah the son of Remaliah, Ahaz the son of Jotham, king of Judah, became king. Ahaz was twenty years old when he became king, and he reigned for sixteen years in Jerusalem; and he did not do what was right in the sight of the LORD his God, as his father David had done. (2 Kings 16:1–2)

I was shocked when I read the phrase "he did not do what was right in the sight of the LORD his God." This was the Old Testament way of saying that this guy did not follow God. Are you kidding me? The king who would bring revival to Judah was raised by a father who did not follow God? How does that happen? Prepare yourself—it gets even more twisted.

> But he walked in the way of the kings of Israel, and he even made his son pass through the fire, in accordance with the abominations of the nations whom the LORD had driven out before the sons of Israel. (2 Kings 16:3)

Did you get that? Ahaz "even made his son pass through the fire." While we don't know for sure, that son could have been Hezekiah. Now I'm even more confused. Not only did Ahaz reject the Lord's rule, but he was also an abusive father. He made his son "pass through the fire."

There is debate over what this phrase means. In rabbinic tradition, passing a child through the fire referred to a ceremony in which the child was sacrificed to an idol by the child's father, resulting either in death or in being scarred for life, both emotionally and physically.[2] Picture Ahaz's son Hezekiah passing through the fire and surviving, but being left with horrible scars that would stay with him for the rest of his life. He would have scars—scars put there by his father on both the inside and the outside.

REDEEMING MAN-MADE SCARS

I'm quite sure that many people can relate to Hezekiah's story. Maybe you're among them. The father who was supposed to tell you how proud he was of you and protect you instead put you in harm's way. The uncle you thought you could trust touched you in private places. The pastor to whom you bared your soul ended up manipulating you. The mother whose affection and approval you craved called you stupid. The parent you thought loved you never dared to say the words out loud. The teacher who was supposed to teach you abused and molested you instead.

You've been injured. You've been wounded. And you still have the scars to tell the story.

You feel more scarred than royal right now. Yet in the midst of those feelings, there is hope. Remember this about Hezekiah: though his earthly father rejected him, there was another Father who accepted him. God took Hezekiah, scars and all, and said, "I see royalty in you. I see a revival happening through you." God saw this boy's scars, the abuse he had suffered in the past, but God also saw his future and his destiny.

If you're reading this book with scars spread across your body, wondering how you can be something special with those marks, remember this: though you may have been rejected, there is another set of eyes on you that sees *more* in you. The eyes of God see deeper and further. God says, "Though you were rejected by your father, you are not rejected by Me."

God has a track record of putting robes on scars. Do you know who is the lead character in God's biggest "robes on scars" story? He is sitting right next to Him in heaven at His right hand. Think about this: the only man-made things in heaven are the scars on Jesus' body. Reigning in heaven right now is the King with a robe of righteousness and some man-made scars. God put the robe on the scars for His Son, and He did it for Hezekiah, and He will do it for you.

PUT A ROBE ON THE SCARS

"Put a robe on your scars" is the story of a child raised in a castle. Hezekiah's father was the influential king of a powerful nation. But even a home like that is not off-limits to scars and wounds. Scars happen because people are selfish and self-seeking. Why are they selfish and self-seeking? Because sin exists. The selfish man who scarred this boy was Hezekiah's own father. "Put a robe on your scars" teaches us not to ignore our past but to use our scars like an old marked-up textbook that reminds us of what we've learned.

"My dad did this to me" and "My dad made me like this" are familiar lines I hear. And that could have been Hezekiah's line. But Hezekiah was different. Instead of grumbling to others about what had been done to him, this young boy who became king at twenty-five years old, treated the scars of the past differently. He held his post for twenty-nine years. And never once does the Bible tell us that during his reign as king, he talked about what his father, Ahaz, had done to him. He decided to put a robe on those scars. The robe was what he was destined to be.

Your robe may be parenting, ministry, marriage, or getting a college degree or even a high school diploma. The robe represents what we are supposed to do and to be, regardless of what life has done to try to stop us.

FROM WOUND TO SCAR

My father was a godly man who was a wisdom resource and a prayer warrior for me in my life. Whenever I found myself in a difficult situation, my first phone call was to

Dad. What do you do when your dad is the scar maker, as was true for Hezekiah? When someone does not have that privilege to call their dad due to a tragic past, you find them going up higher and calling on their heavenly Father. Throughout the reign of Hezekiah, it's no accident that we see this king cry out to God so often. The Bible makes his prayer life familiar to us. We are seeing that people who walk toward the healing of scars continually find themselves coming back to their Healer, their heavenly Father.

Isaiah 37–39 shares two overwhelming moments in Hezekiah's life—situations for which, for me, my father would have been my first call. In these cases, Hezekiah's first call was to his heavenly Father. In the first instance, the Israelites were up against a large, fierce Assyrian army that was threatening to invade the nation during Hezekiah's reign. When Hezekiah received the horrible news in letter form, he "went up to the house of the LORD and spread it out before the LORD. Hezekiah prayed to the LORD" (Isaiah 37:14–15). Not only did God hear Hezekiah's prayer, but he responded so fast and decisively that 185,000 Assyrians were killed in one night by just one of heaven's angels (Isaiah 37:36). Hezekiah knew he had to call on his Father because God was the only father he could call on.

I was recently diagnosed with prostate cancer. Thank God it was not alarming for the doctor, but it was alarming for me. The first call I desperately wanted to make was to my father, but he had passed in 2000. This is one of those shocking reports for which a boy needs a strong father. But I learned from the scarred king what to do when a person's father isn't there for them—they go to their heavenly Father. I did that because Hezekiah did that.

The boy who had a robe on his scars was diagnosed with a terminal illness and told he would die (Isaiah 38:1). As soon as the diagnosis came, "Hezekiah turned his face to the wall and prayed to the LORD" (38:2). The God who healed the boy of his wounds would also be the God who would heal him of his illness. I was fatherless at a vulnerable moment in my later life. And Hezekiah knew what it felt like to be fatherless, since his father had forsaken him. Here is the good news about God as told in Psalm 68:5: He is "a father of the fatherless." Whether Hezekiah was facing down a large army, an incurable sickness, or an abusive father, he always found healing in his heavenly Father. God sent an angel against an invading army. God sent healing for an incurable disease. And God put a robe on the tragic scars caused by his father. Wounded people tell people about their wounds, but when that wound becomes a scar, scarred people find themselves talking to God more than talking to people.

There is a difference between scars and wounds. A scar is a wound that has been healed. A wound that has not yet turned into a scar is a highly sensitive place on the body. You can minister from scars but not wounds.

I have seen people try to get to their destiny with wounds. They don't stay there long. Staying in woundedness in your journey toward your destiny is not an option. Wounds must become scars.

Hezekiah's story has similarities to the story we'll unfold in the next chapter. We must introduce it here because it guides us toward the secret of turning our wounds into scars. It's the story of another leader who was wounded and scarred by his family and also got a robe put on those scars. His name was Joseph.

Let me briefly take you to one scene in Joseph's life. A robe has been placed on the scars his brothers caused. Joseph was beginning to give us a glimpse of a wound that was turning into a scar. In Genesis 45, Joseph stood in front of his scar makers. And there Joseph gave us his secret to healing—a secret I believe Hezekiah experienced as well.

And Joseph said to his brothers, "I am Joseph! Is my father still alive?" But his brothers could not answer him, for they were terrified in his presence.

Then Joseph said to his brothers, "Please come closer to me." And they came closer. And he said, "I am your brother Joseph, whom you sold to Egypt. Now do not be grieved or angry with yourselves because you sold me here, for God sent me ahead of you to save lives. For the famine has been in the land these two years, and there are still five years in which there will be neither plowing nor harvesting. So God sent me ahead of you to ensure for you a remnant on the earth, and to keep you alive by a great deliverance. Now, therefore, it was not you who sent me here, but God; and He has made me a father to Pharaoh and lord of all his household, and ruler over all the land of Egypt. Hurry and go up to my father, and say to him, 'This is what your son Joseph says: "God has made me lord of all Egypt; come down to me, do not delay."'" (Genesis 45:3–9)

The secret is found in one word as Joseph faced his attackers—one word that Joseph uses over and over again to tell us the wound is now a scar. It's the word *God*. Look at how many times Joseph said *God* as he recounted his story with his brothers. Joseph came to the realization that God had sent him to Egypt, not his brothers. He kept replacing the painful deeds of his brothers with the providential hand of God.

I'm convinced that this is the difference between someone who speaks from a wound and someone who speaks from a scar. A person who is still wounded will talk about the people who hurt them; by contrast, those who have a robe on their scars now talk about God all the time. They see God in their painful journey. You don't hear a list of people's names; you hear one name—God.

By the way, there's no problem with you telling your scar story as long as it ends with Jesus and isn't just your song of bitterness at the people who have hurt you.

I don't think we realize how God readies a person to do His will. The film *The Voyage of the Dawn Treader* had it right when it added a line spoken by Reepicheep during the scene where Eustace has become a dragon: "Hardships often prepare ordinary people for an extraordinary destiny."[3] God is raising up a broken and scarred generation to be His leaders. Wounds must turn to scars. And then, in a beautiful turn of events, those scars get a robe.

Christianity boldly and unashamedly goes backward to get us moving forward. Simply put, God deals with our past, even if we won't. Most times, these past memories are painful, but pain does not mean we refuse to confront them or we declare them off-limits. We all tend to want to avoid pain, especially pain we haven't thought about for a while. And yet our future can be brighter when our past is resolved and understood.

When we step into a doctor's office, the doctor wants to know where it hurts, not where it feels good. Jesus comes as the Great Physician and deals with "where it hurts"— because where it hurts is exactly what needs to be healed. And most of the time, what needs to be healed is what has happened to us. God shows us that the past doesn't have to cripple us or hinder us. Those past pains can actually make us the people of character we were meant to be.

No one escapes pain in life. Everyone must deal with it, but not everyone does. Everyone goes through it, but not everyone gets over it. Most people are so locked into what someone has done to them that they lose their ability to be what God has created them to be. Christianity does not exempt us from pain, but it gives us the tools to get through our pain. Augustine put it this way: "In my deepest wound

I saw your glory, and it dazzled me."[4] We need more people dazzled in the wound and not destroyed by it.

FROM CURSE TO BLESSING

If all we see is Hezekiah in his royal robe in 2 Kings 18, we only know part of his story. We're seeing the throne but not the process. I can imagine someone saying to Hezekiah, "One day, I would like to be a king like you," and the young king responding by lifting up his robes and saying, "Let me show you what I had to go through to get here."

There is not a person on the planet who reaches adulthood unscathed by people, situations, failures, disappointments, and, frankly, just life itself. Life wounds and scars people.

Every person comes into Christianity with baggage. Every piece of luggage represents an event from their painful past. That excess baggage was never meant to be hauled around from place to place for "show and tell." Sadly, that's what is happening today. The excess baggage has made victims out of people instead of helping them become people of character. We need to see every piece of luggage as a blackboard, a teaching moment.

Every person has their robe waiting. But every person must make an important decision: Will I show off my scars, or will I show off my robe? The choice is ours. God really can take the most painful time of our lives and bring something amazing out of it. And He does it because of His love for us. Deuteronomy 23:5 describes it like this: "The LORD your God turned the curse into a blessing for you because the LORD your God loves you."

God turned the curse into a blessing for my friend Kevin. God did it for Hezekiah. God can do it for you. It's that "turn" that gets you closer to what God has called you to be, not what other people's actions keep you stuck on. In the next chapter, we'll learn about someone who navigated the "turn" from curse to blessing better than anyone else—Joseph, son of Jacob.

DISCUSSION QUESTIONS

1. What hurdle do you face in turning a wound into a scar? And how might you deal with that hurdle?

2. When someone shares their wound story, what can you do first to start "scar ministry" and help them toward healing?

3. Briefly share a personal story of hurt without using the offending person's name. Tell it from God's perspective so you can testify to how God used that hurtful time to change you.

CHAPTER 2

TRAINING FOR GREATNESS WITH JOSEPH

There is a long tradition that those who were
used the most by God waited the longest.
R. T. Kendall, *Pure Joy*

Some time ago, our oldest daughter, Anna, came home from elementary school and immediately begged me to take her to the local park so she could train on the running track. I asked her, "What are you training for? You're only seven."

She said, "We are having our school field day. I am training for fourth place."

"What?" I shouted. "Training for fourth place?" I was dumbfounded. Anna has always been competitive and will work hard to get what she wants. Yet here she was, setting a goal to win fourth place.

She then said, "I found out that the ribbon for fourth place is pink, and that's my favorite color."

And suddenly it all made sense.

My daughter aside, does anyone really train for any other ribbon but the blue one you receive for winning first place? No one does, at least not knowingly. Who dreams of coming in second? Who dreams of winning that red ribbon?

Turns out, the Bible tells of a person who dreamed a red-ribbon dream—for him to become the prime minister of the most powerful nation on the planet at that time. His name was Joseph, and his story is found in Genesis 37.

WHEN WE'RE MAD AT GOD

"You can't have a relationship without any fights, but you can make your relationship worth the fight."[1] All relationships go through hell at times. Real relationships get through it. One of the hardest decisions we face in life is choosing whether to walk away from a relationship or to try harder.

But here is the big question: What do you do when the relationship that is giving you problems is your relationship with God? What do you do when you feel God has let you down? When you feel betrayed by Him? When you feel wronged?

There are times when God makes me really, really angry. It's not because of a defect in Him, but rather because of a defect in me. He becomes the target of my frustration. When we suffer or go through pain, we want to blame someone, and the first person to blame is usually God.

Remember the movie *Bruce Almighty*? Jim Carrey portrays a television reporter who constantly complains about God. At one point, he says, "God is a mean kid sitting on an anthill with a magnifying glass, and I'm the ant. He could fix my life in five minutes if He wanted to, but He'd rather burn off my feelers and watch me squirm."[2]

To prove to Bruce that He knows what He's doing, God (played by Morgan Freeman) offers to let Bruce try to run the world in His place. Bruce soon realizes the enormity and complexity of God's work, particularly in answering prayers.

Jim Carrey's prayer doesn't bother me because his prayer reflects the way people in the Bible prayed. To pray is to be honest with God. The Bible has many examples of people telling God, in raw and unpolished ways, that they are frustrated with Him.

Job said in Job 7:16–21 (TLB):

"I hate my life. Oh, leave me alone for these few remaining days. What is mere man that you should spend your time persecuting him? Must you be his inquisitor every morning and test him every moment of the day? Why won't you leave me alone—even long enough to spit?

"Has my sin harmed you, O God, watcher of mankind? Why have you made me your target, and made my life so heavy a burden to me? Why not just pardon my sin and take it all away? For all too soon I'll lie down in the dust and die, and when you look for me, I shall be gone."

David said in Psalm 13:1–2 (TLB), "How long will you forget me, Lord? Forever? How long will you look the other way when I am in need? How long must I be hiding daily anguish in my heart? How long shall my enemy have the upper hand?"

And then my favorite is Moses, who said in Numbers 11:11 (NABRE), "Why do you treat your servant so badly?"

All of these verses are prayers, which means these things are directed to God. The pray-ers are just being real, and at times raw, with God.

Something about these prayers doesn't drive God from them but brings Him closer to them. When I need a doctor, I show them and tell them where the pain is. I don't show them the places I'm healthy but rather the places where it hurts. Why pretend and hide the hurts and wounds? God sees them already.

Some time ago, I read a book with a title I love. In fact, the title made me read it. It was called *May I Hate God?* and was written by a Christian counselor. The author spoke of the people he counseled who felt let down by God. It's during the journey to your dream that you get exhausted and exasperated and ask, "May I hate God?" Saint Teresa of Ávila's words during her tough times have come to my mind many times on this journey: "Lord, if this is the way you treat your friends, it's no surprise you have so few of them."[3]

I believe Joseph, the son of the biblical patriarch Jacob, had to face these thoughts. There were probably points in Joseph's life when he asked, "May I hate God?" God gave him a dream about the future that showed people bowing before him, but what God didn't show him was the process he'd have to go through to get to that end. Joseph was going to experience some things that would have him hating God's curriculum. God must know that if He were to show us what His training looked like, we would all be tempted to abort the journey. In Joseph's case, knowing the process would have meant that the end result was no longer a dream but rather a nightmare.

TRAINING INTENSIVE

If you are going to train someone to become the second-in-command of the planet, what would you do to train them? Have them read leadership books? Get their Harvard MBA? Get some experience and coaching from a high-level executive?

God chose for Joseph a three-course curriculum to

prepare him for leadership. One Christian apologist put it this way: "God does it his way. . . . He trained Joseph in a desert to use him in a palace."[4] God has a curriculum. I don't have to say, "I love it," but I can say, "It's the most effective training." Joseph's end is going to be extraordinary, but his curriculum will be filled with hardships.

Here are God's three courses: (1) You will be betrayed by the closest people in your life. (2) You will be accused of something and you won't be able to defend yourself. And finally, (3) you will be promised something and the person doesn't deliver what they say they will. Think of those three courses—betrayal, accusation, and broken promises. This would be Joseph's curriculum.

Do these three tests sound familiar to anyone? Let's see how Joseph navigates each test and how God uses them to get him to his dream.

COURSE 1: BETRAYAL

I've heard it said that tough times don't define you; they refine you—and betrayal is one of the toughest times to go through. Betrayal is not just a tragedy; it's a classroom.

Why is this a course in God's school? What does it actually produce? It produces greater trust in God, and it takes our eyes off people.

Betrayal isn't painful simply because of what we go

through. It's painful because of who puts us through it. David described his betrayal like this in Psalm 55:12–14 (NIV):

> If an enemy were insulting me,
>> I could endure it;
> if a foe were rising against me,
>> I could hide.
> But it is you, a man like myself,
>> my companion, my close friend,
> with whom I once enjoyed sweet fellowship
>> at the house of God,
> as we walked about
>> among the worshipers.

My dear friend and youth communicator Winkie Pratney said it this way: "Hurt is proportional to intimacy."[5] In other words, the closer a person is to us, the less it takes for them to hurt us.

Small betrayals become huge when the person is close to us. Jesus faced betrayal with Judas. David faced it with Ahithophel, his counselor. And Paul faced it with Alexander. For us, it's the person who promised to pay us back and never did. The person we trusted with personal information in confidence, and then they went public with it. The guy in church who said he could do the work on our house for a good "Christian" price, and now we have half a project. It's the person who invited us, and then rescinded the invitation; who told us we'd be their maid of honor, and then someone else was; who said, "I'll call you back soon," and never did. It can be small betrayals or large ones, but the hurt and pain still go deep.

Joseph was betrayed by his own brothers. Ouch!

A FULL BAG

Joseph had a dream. He never thought sharing his dream with the closest people in his life—his brothers—would go really badly for him.

> Joseph had a dream, and when he told it to his brothers, they hated him all the more. He said to them, "Listen to this dream I had: We were binding sheaves of grain out in the field when suddenly my sheaf rose and stood upright, while your sheaves gathered around mine and bowed down to it."
>
> His brothers said to him, "Do you intend to reign over us? Will you actually rule us?" And they hated him all the more because of his dream and what he had said. (Genesis 37:5–8 NIV)

Something about this dream provoked deep emotion in Joseph's brothers. They already disliked him because their father showed him preferential treatment. According to Genesis 37:4 (NIV), "When his brothers saw that their father loved him more than any of them, they hated him and could not speak a kind word to him." When Joseph started dreaming, their dislike for him was taken to a new level.

When I was a child, my father would sometimes say to us, "The bag is getting full," which meant one of us was doing or saying things we weren't supposed to and was really close to being disciplined. That was our warning shot.

Joseph should have realized the bag was getting full, but he didn't. So when he had a second dream, he went ahead and told his brothers all about it. That was all the ammunition Joseph's brothers needed.

The Genesis account tells us that one day, Joseph sought out his brothers on his father's orders. The bag was full and overflowing. As soon as they spotted Joseph on the horizon, the brothers saw an opportunity:

> So when Joseph came to his brothers, they stripped him of his robe—the ornate robe he was wearing—and they took him and threw him into the cistern. The cistern was empty; there was no water in it.
>
> As they sat down to eat their meal, they looked up and saw a caravan of Ishmaelites coming from Gilead. Their camels were loaded with spices, balm and myrrh, and they were on their way to take them down to Egypt.
>
> Judah said to his brothers, "What will we gain if we kill our brother and cover up his blood? Come, let's sell him to the Ishmaelites and not lay our hands on him; after all, he is our brother, our own flesh and blood." His brothers agreed.

So when the Midianite merchants came by, his brothers pulled Joseph up out of the cistern and sold him for twenty shekels of silver to the Ishmaelites, who took him to Egypt. (Genesis 37:23–28 NIV)

DEEP WOUNDS

A. W. Tozer once said, "It is doubtful whether God can bless a man greatly until He has hurt him deeply."[6] This is what Joseph's brothers did to him. For Joseph, this deep hurt was the wounds from being thrown into a pit— wounds that I have to believe were not just from the pit on the outside but also from the brothers on the inside.

Solomon wrote, "Sometimes it takes a painful experience to make us change our ways" (Proverbs 20:30 GNT). God was going to use this painful event in Joseph's life to change him and prepare him for the future Joseph had dreamed about. William Secker, a nineteenth-century Puritan writer, said this: "If Joseph does not become the prisoner of Egypt then he would not become the governor of Egypt."[7]

Joseph's journey to Egypt was God's plan. Joseph's betrayal by his brothers would be the mechanism to get him to Egypt. The dream was going to become a reality in Egypt decades later. But Joseph was going to have to learn the lesson of being betrayed by the closest people in his life while not letting his bitterness go with him into his prime minister office.

When we are hurt, it is easy to isolate ourselves. We can

become skeptical of people and unwilling to let anyone get close to us. This can be dangerous and keep us from the important friendships we need on our journey.

How do we protect our hearts from being skeptical or cynical and putting up walls so people won't get close and we won't get hurt again? How do we make betrayal a lesson instead of a prison? The knee-jerk response is to say, "I don't need any friends. I can do this by myself." I don't think we can grow or get to where we're supposed to be without relationships. And I don't think we can have close relationships without experiencing betrayal. The person who chooses to protect their heart from the school of hurt by keeping people away is dangerous. Listen to C. S. Lewis's words from *The Four Loves*:

> To love at all is to be vulnerable. Love anything, and your heart will certainly be wrung and possibly be broken. If you want to make sure of keeping it intact, you must give it to no one, not even to an animal. Wrap it carefully round with hobbies and little luxuries; avoid all entanglements; lock it up safe in the casket or coffin of your selfishness. But in that casket—safe, dark, motionless, airless—it will change. It will not be broken; it will become unbreakable, impenetrable, irredeemable.[8]

To love is to be vulnerable. To not trust people again is to harden our hearts. We cannot have close friendships without a few betrayals and scars to keep our hearts softened.

Betrayal can put our focus in the right place. Our wounds turn our eyes toward God. That's what Joseph was learning—to see God's plan and movement even in betrayal.

TAKEN

Genesis 39:1 says the Ishmaelites "had taken" Joseph to Egypt. Remember the movie *Taken* with Liam Neeson? Kim, the daughter of the main character, Bryan, goes overseas and is taken by a child trafficking ring. The rest of the movie focuses on Bryan's determination to find his daughter and get her home. "Taken" means she was kidnapped. "Taken" means it took place against her will.

Joseph was *taken* too. The only difference is that Liam Neeson wasn't out there actively seeking to rescue him. God was in heaven superintending the whole process and saw everything that was happening, but He was not on a mission to pull him out prematurely. In God's eyes, this was a school and not a detour.

Egypt wasn't a particularly good place to go at that time. Whenever you read in the Bible that someone has gone "down to Egypt," it's a symbol of bondage, a bad choice, or dangerous living. For Joseph, his journey to Egypt was not done by choice but against his will.

We've gotten ourselves into certain messes because of our own disobedience, bad choices, or failure to seek wisdom. And then there are situations, like Joseph's, that leave us thinking, *I didn't sign up for this. This isn't my fault. I didn't cause this.* Someone else's sin, poor choices, or selfishness brought us there.

I know a lot of *taken* people. Some of us have been *taken* into debt because of a spouse's irresponsible money management. Some of us have been *taken* into different states because our spouse thought a move was a way to advance their career. Some of us have children who have *taken* us into fear and worry every night because of their lifestyle. Some of us are empty nesters who have been *taken* back into parenting because of a child's promiscuity and the children who were born out of wedlock. Some of us have been *taken* into strained coexistence for the children's sake.

Remember this: we can be *taken* and still be *blessed.* The blessing of God is on His people, not on locations. Don't miss that. No matter where we are geographically, we just need to remember that God is with us, even in a place to which we've been taken. Joseph was taken but Joseph was blessed. Joseph had God with him. Listen to the next verse after Joseph's *taken* verse:

> Now Joseph had been taken down to Egypt; and Potiphar, an Egyptian officer of Pharaoh, the captain of the bodyguard, bought him from the Ishmaelites, who had taken him down there. And the LORD was with Joseph, so he became a successful man. And he was in the house of his master, the Egyptian. (Genesis 39:1–2)

If the Lord is with us, it means He is with us wherever we go—that is, in our *entire* journey. Joseph didn't realize that his presence in Egypt would mean he was in his final residence. He would never go back to Israel, his homeland. Egypt is where he would be buried, but Egypt is the place where he would be a savior and fulfill his dream. On paper, Joseph was *taken*, but in heaven's perspective, Joseph was exactly where he was supposed to be.

COURSE 2: ACCUSATION

In the aftermath of being *taken*, Joseph is still blessed, and his job is going great. He is sold to an official named Potiphar. This is how the Bible describes Joseph as an employee and his relationship with his employer:

> Now his master saw that the LORD was with him and that the LORD made all that he did prosper in his hand. So Joseph found favor in his sight and became his personal servant; and he made him overseer over his house, and put him in charge of all that he owned. It came about that from the time he made him overseer in his house and over all that he owned, the LORD blessed the Egyptian's house on account of Joseph; so the LORD's blessing was upon all that he owned, in the house and in the field. So he left Joseph in charge of everything that he owned; and with him there he did not concern

himself with anything except the food which he ate. (Genesis 39:3–6)

But then the new curriculum started. Joseph left betrayal and entered into the accusation classroom. Someone at the job site accused Joseph of sexual advances.

For the past few years, the issue of sexual advances (both false accusations and true cases of abuse) has been headlining the news. It is happening in the church world, in the government, and in Hollywood. People are losing their jobs, their credibility, and their future over this issue. It has been an epidemic that is just coming to light. This isn't new; it's just been lurking underneath the surface.

The Bible tells us that Potiphar's wife took notice of Joseph's appearance and made sexual advances toward him. Joseph never flinched. He refused on two grounds— his boss and his God:

> But he refused and said to his master's wife, "Look, with me here, my master does not concern himself with anything in the house, and he has put me in charge of all that he owns. There is no one greater in this house than I, and he has withheld nothing from me except you, because you are his wife. How then could I do this great evil, and sin against God?" (Genesis 39:8–9)

Mrs. Potiphar was not deterred by these two compelling grounds. She was relentless. The Bible says she approached him "day after day" (Genesis 39:10), refusing to stop until she got her prey. But Joseph was determined. Unfortunately, so was Mrs. Potiphar. She was so determined that she took the advances from words to actions:

> Now it happened one day that he went into the house to do his work, and none of the people of the household was there inside. So she grabbed him by his garment, saying, "Sleep with me!" But he left his garment in her hand and fled, and went outside. (Genesis 39:11–12)

Mrs. Potiphar made the advances, but Joseph refused. Here come the lies and accusations that never made the news in Egypt. She called it rape when in fact it was sexual purity.

> When she saw that he had left his garment in her hand and had fled outside, she called to the men of her household and said to them, "See, he has brought in a Hebrew to us to make fun of us; he came in to me to sleep with me, and I screamed. When he heard that I raised my voice and screamed, he left his garment beside me and fled and went outside." So she left his garment beside her until his master came home. Then she spoke to him with these words: "The Hebrew slave, whom you brought to us, came in to me to make fun of me; but when I raised my voice and screamed, he left his garment beside me and fled outside."
> Now when his master heard the words of his wife

which she spoke to him, saying, "This is what your slave did to me," his anger burned. So Joseph's master took him and put him into the prison, the place where the king's prisoners were confined; and he was there in the prison. (Genesis 39:13–20)

Joseph did what was right and he now was the one getting penalized. Joseph's story is the story of a young man who won over sexual temptation.

We hear so many stories of failure, but Joseph's is an amazing example of sexual purity for all the right reasons. But at the end of the test, there were no party favors, no purity rings—only an accusation and a prison sentence.

A JUST REWARD?

Wow, where was God in this situation? I thought God rewarded purity.

We all face times when we don't understand God's process and grow angry with Him, when we feel that we should've gotten a party but instead got a prison cell. We did what was right, but we were wrongly accused.

I remember those feelings on my journey. The words that gave me strength came from Joseph's father, Jacob, when his uncle Laban had falsely accused him: "My honesty will answer for me later" (Genesis 30:33). There have been days when I had to whisper these words to my soul. You may want to say them right now. Joseph certainly had to say them.

TRUST GOD'S JUSTICE

Remember what we said earlier: God's blessing is not on a location, but on His people. Joseph was blessed even when he'd been *taken*, and he was blessed even when he had been *accused*:

> So Joseph's master took him and put him into the prison, the place where the king's prisoners were confined; and he was there in the prison. But the LORD was with Joseph and extended kindness to him, and gave him favor in the sight of the warden of the prison. (Genesis 39:20–21)

"The LORD was with Joseph" should bring comfort to our lives. When you are accused and you can't defend yourself, God will be with you. God was with Joseph to teach Joseph. What was God speaking to him? God was teaching him that God is the best person to defend us. Our knee-jerk reaction may be to explain, defend, blog, post, or tweet. My mind goes back to one of Augustine's prayers that I had to embrace: "Lord, deliver me from this lust of always vindicating myself."[9] Defending myself is an even harder lust to break than sensuality. Augustine calls it a lust to vindicate myself. In those moments when you want to go public with your story, pause. Let God defend you. Your honesty will answer for you later.

There is an important thought I want you to keep in mind, though: the truth doesn't always have to be told in words. You never hear of Joseph's "rape" story getting corrected. I wonder if, when Joseph rose to power, people muttered, "Isn't that the guy that raped Potiphar's wife?" Even more astounding is that Joseph didn't vindicate himself when he had the power and position to do so. It seems God wanted to vindicate him with the success and progress of his walk instead.

COURSE 3: BROKEN PROMISES

As we grow up, we learn all sorts of ways to make a promise. When I was a kid, we sealed every promise with, "Cross my heart, hope to die, stick a needle in my eye." Then came pinky promises. My kids don't hook pinkies; instead, they make a cross with their index fingers and make a "Jesus promise." When you "Jesus promise," you have to come through and keep your word.

When we break a promise, we indict our character. To say we will do something and not do it looks bad on us. So many promises we make involve the future: promised jobs, promised positions, promised raises, promises to get married, promises to stay together for better or for worse, promises to check in again tomorrow, promises that we'll get together again soon. The list goes on and on, and every one of us has had a promise broken.

When promises regarding our future plans are broken, we're crushed. Experiencing broken promises is the subject of Joseph's last class in his curriculum to fulfill his dream.

This final course starts in Genesis 40. Joseph is in prison on a false accusation of rape. Two new inmates are brought to Joseph's prison. But these aren't ordinary inmates. These two men, a cupbearer and a baker, came from the palace and were sentenced by Pharaoh himself. Genesis 40:3 says they were put in the same place that Joseph was.

Nothing is coincidental with God. He will connect us with the right people to get us to where we need to be. No one could have scripted this better than God.

Everything changed for Joseph—and his relationship with these two men—when the cupbearer and the baker both had dreams. Joseph noticed the men were sad and asked them what was wrong. Joseph listened to their dreams and interpreted them—one of them would receive capital punishment, and the other would be restored to his job.

Things played out just as Joseph had said. Three days later, the baker was executed and the cupbearer got his job back. Joseph asked the cupbearer to remember him once he got reinstated to his job. But Joseph was forgotten and left in prison.

For two more years Joseph was left to think about the broken promise as he sat in his prison cell. But God was preparing to use this broken promise. Joseph was going to learn what David said in Psalm 108:12–13: "Deliverance by man is worthless. Through God we will do valiantly."

I think God allows people we trust to break promises, even unknowingly, to teach us that our future is not based on what people do but rather on what God permits in His perfect timing.

GRADUATION DAY

One day it all changed for Joseph. Graduation day had come! Guess who had a dream? Pharaoh, the leader of Egypt. Guess who suggested that Joseph should come and interpret the dream? A cupbearer suddenly remembered a promise made to a Hebrew prisoner who had an extraordinary gift.

Pharaoh had a dream of a fourteen-year period in the land of Egypt, and it was prophetic (Genesis 41). He saw fat and thin cows, but Joseph saw seven years of plenty and seven years of famine. He instructed Pharaoh on what to do in the land to prepare for those famine years. Pharaoh wisely recognized that Joseph was a wise man—the right person to handle this situation—and made Joseph the number two man of Egypt.

Joseph was training all this time for second place. Now he got the red ribbon. And that red ribbon was really tough preparation for something else—reuniting with his brothers.

We then get this great verse: "Now Joseph was thirty years old when he stood in the presence of Pharaoh, king of Egypt. And Joseph went out from the presence of Pharaoh and went through all the land of Egypt" (Genesis 41:46). God's curriculum took thirteen years. God saw those years as the preparation for that very moment.

Who would have thought that this curriculum was the way to the throne for Joseph? Not me. But God did.

Your disappointments right now may really be part of God's curriculum. What may seem like a setback is really a move forward. One unknown pundit said, "Getting over a painful experience is much like crossing monkey bars. You have to let go at some point in order to move forward."[10] Joseph would have to let go of any bitterness because of betrayal, accusation, and broken promises in order to move forward. Remember R. T. Kendall's words from the beginning of this chapter? "There is a long tradition that those who were used the most by God waited the longest."[11]

DISCUSSION QUESTIONS

1. *Betrayal* is such a strong word. Can you describe the difference between betrayal and hurt?
2. Can you recall a promise you have broken but have not fixed? What small actions can you take to start the healing process?
3. Joseph could have cleared his name as a criminal, but he didn't. What are some advantages to living forward and not revisiting the past?

CHAPTER 3

NAVIGATING BLANK SPACES WITH ABRAHAM

Big doors swing on little hinges.
W. Clement Stone, *Believe and Achieve*

More Christians are living in China today than in the United States. According to *Charisma* magazine, thirty thousand Chinese people turn to Christ every day.[1] And that revival traces its roots to the fifty-one years spent by a man named James Hudson Taylor bringing the gospel through the China Inland Mission.

The work was slow and arduous. Taylor suffered from illness, struggled to retain funding for his mission, encountered threats to his life, and faced difficulties communicating the gospel across seemingly insurmountable language and cultural barriers. Upon learning that the mission's premises in Shanghai had been destroyed in a fire, Taylor was tempted to give it up. "I had not then learned," he records, "to think of God as the One Great Circumstance in whom we live and move and have our being, and of all lesser circumstances as necessarily the kindest, wisest, best, because either ordered or permitted by Him. Hence my disappointment and trial were very great."[2] But he persisted, and 150 years later, his work is still shaking the planet. Taylor attributed this success to what he referred to as the little things. The big thing is happening in China today because Hudson Taylor did little things faithfully every day.

In my experience, when we feel like nothing is happening, nothing could be further from the truth. When we say, "Nothing is happening," what we mean is that what we are doing seems to have nothing to do with what we want to be doing in the future. It refers to being stuck doing little, seemingly insignificant things when we want to accomplish great feats—when we want to move forward, but traffic is at a standstill. How many times do we look around as we drive and shout, "What in the world is holding us up? Is it a wreck? Is it a construction zone? We should be moving by now." Life is like that. We get stuck behind other people. It seems like everyone else is ahead of us, moving forward, and we're stuck in life's traffic jam doing a lot of nothing.

BLANK SPACES

"A little thing is a little thing; but faithfulness in little things is a great thing," Hudson Taylor said.[3] In what you are seeing as a traffic jam, your constant tapping the brake with your foot is really an accelerator taking you faster and closer to your destiny. I believe God's curriculum for His people is filled with a lot of bumper-to-bumper traffic jams. Taylor called them "little things"; I call them "blank spaces."

In the blank spaces, we feel like nothing is happening that is worth talking about. It's the "same old, same old"— get up, get the children ready, get yourself ready, make breakfast, get everyone out of the house, work all day, come home, eat dinner, spend time with the family, watch TV, go to bed, and then do the same thing again the next day.

The blank spaces are the daily things we have to do— the things that cause people to call us responsible. Blank space involves doing the things we are supposed to do—the things that may seem redundant, boring, and unworthy of notice. Blank-space stuff goes in the integrity and faithfulness categories. No one ever notices; everyone only expects.

God's journey for each of us seems to have a lot of blank spaces. We don't think anything noteworthy is happening during these times, but God thinks otherwise. He thinks it's all worth noticing, and He even records periods of blank spaces in His Word.

There's a conspicuous blank space in the Bible that I want to draw your attention to. The Bible even tells us how long this blank space was. There are no words in the blank space because no words were needed. There isn't much talking going on, but rather just a lot of little things being done. This blank space probably doesn't measure even half an inch, but its actual timeline spans more than a decade. It's found between Genesis 16 and 17. The people in the blank space are Abram and Sarai. At his point, their blank space catapulted their lives to an epic event. They trusted the process, and it paid off unexpectedly.

THE SPACE BETWEEN OUR MISTAKES AND OUR PURPOSE

In Genesis 16, we see what happens when we try to make God's promises happen faster than when God intended. We try to manipulate God's calendar to align with our iCal. That's what Abram and Sarai tried to do in Genesis 16. They were promised in Genesis 15 that they would have a miracle child—a *miracle*, to be sure, because they were way past childbearing age.

When we get to Genesis 16, we find that Abram and Sarai had grown impatient. God was moving too slowly for them. So Abram and Sarai looked at their old bodies and said, "Impossible! We need to help God make it happen." They concocted a scheme in which Abram would sleep with their maid, Hagar, and her pregnancy would result in their miracle child. This was a *big mistake*—for all of us! It was *catastrophic*. I don't use that word frivolously; it really was. It's a blunder that still reverberates today. When we hear about turmoil in the Middle East, this couple and their bad decision represent the starting point.

Now let's fast-forward past the mistake to Genesis 17. This chapter is epic, pointing to the highlight of Abram's life—the new covenant that God had promised to make with him that would continue through the generations. This section of the Bible is referenced often in the New Testament. Echoes of it are found in Romans, Galatians, and Hebrews.

Sixteen was the worst chapter of Abram's life. Seventeen was the greatest chapter of Abraham's life (see Genesis 17:5 for Abram's name change). And between the two is the blank space that Abraham had to go through as part of God's process. Here's how the blank space looks:

Genesis 16:16: Abram was eighty-six years old when Hagar bore Ishmael to him.

Genesis 17:1: Now when Abram was ninety-nine years old, the Lord appeared to Abram and said to him, "I am God Almighty; walk before Me, and be blameless."

When the Bible gives someone's age, take note to see if the text mentions that person's age again later on. Through these age markers, the Scriptures are depicting a journey. We can see that thirteen years pass between the end of Genesis 16 and the beginning of Genesis 17. That's thirteen years of blank spaces. Thirteen years during which there didn't seem to be anything good enough to record about Abraham's life.

We've all had a chapter 16—that time in our lives we regret and wish we could do over. It's a decision we'd like to rethink and choose the other option. It's something we're still paying for today—child support, a criminal record, a child out of wedlock, a scar on our body we never intended to be there, or a scar on our soul that is with us every day.

CHAPTER 16 DECISIONS

Maybe your chapter 16 was an abortion decision, or maybe you're considering an abortion right now. Here's a thought: Would you consider recommending abortion in the following four situations?

1. A preacher and his wife are very poor and already have fourteen kids. She has just found out she's pregnant with number fifteen. Considering their poverty and the

excessive world population, would you consider recommending she get an abortion?

2. The father is sick with sniffles and the mother has tuberculosis. They have four children—the first is blind, the second dead, the third deaf, and the fourth has TB. She finds out she's pregnant again. Given the extreme situation, would you consider recommending abortion?

3. A White man raped a thirteen-year-old Black girl, which resulted in a pregnancy. If you were her parents, would you consider recommending abortion?

4. An unmarried teen girl is pregnant. Her fiancé is not the father of the baby, and he's very upset. Would you consider recommending abortion?

- In the first case, you've killed John Wesley, one of the great evangelists of the eighteenth century.
- In the second case, you've killed Ludwig von Beethoven.
- In the third case, you've killed Ethel Waters, the great gospel singer.
- If you said yes to the fourth scenario, you've just declared the murder of Jesus![4]

"Abortion is advocated only by persons who themselves have already been born," said Ronald Reagan [5] Even if you made a chapter 16 decision, remember that the next season is when you'll live most of your life. Regardless of the poor choices Abraham made in chapter 16, God didn't take chapter 17 away from him. Our mistakes are not deal-breakers. There is hope.

Chapter 17 is the reason we were born. It's what we were made for. It's that moment in our lives that we get to do what God made us to do.

How do we get from chapter 16, the horrible decisions, to chapter 17, the fulfillment of our dreams? This is where the blank spaces come into play. They help us move toward our dreams in spite of our horrible mistakes.

NAVIGATING THE BLANK SPACES WELL

The thirteen years that Abraham has nothing written about his life of faith represent a life lived before an audience of one—God. It's a life that was lived without the notice and applause of people. And that is our life today.

We need to be reminded of three things about these blank-space seasons in our life:

1. Little things matter—so don't grow weary.
2. Perseverance is always promoted—so don't give up.
3. Your greatest chapter comes suddenly—so get ready.

LITTLE THINGS MATTER

What did that blank space mean for Abraham? This is where Abraham took responsibility for his dumb mistake. He did not place blame on others. He did not walk out on the child and simply send a check each month. He had a baby and had to take care of that baby. In today's terms, we would say Abraham was changing Ishmael's diapers and teaching him how to speak and walk. He was rocking him to sleep at night. He was heating up his milk. That was his life. And he was doing it with—wait for it—no applause. No cheering. No one watching except God.

And that baby was not the miracle baby he had been promised. Think about that. Abraham was taking care of a baby who wasn't to be his future or have anything to do with the promise he was given by God. Yet Ishmael was still *his* baby. Perhaps he had Abraham's eyes, his nose, his hair. He had Abraham's DNA, but he didn't have God's endorsement.

It wasn't Ishmael's fault; it was the result of Abraham's blunder. Abraham had to look at his stupidity every day in the face of that precious baby and realize, *You are not my problem . . . I am my problem.* It would have been easy to make that little boy the target of his angst. It would have likely been a challenge to love a son who caused him so much inconvenience.

The challenge in this season of your life is to stay faithful, even when it seems like what you do isn't making a difference. You may feel like you're wasting time and you should be doing something more meaningful. But it's those little things that matter most in the blank spaces. You *are* making a difference. When you feel like you're stuck, remember these powerful words: "Isn't it funny how day by day nothing changes, but when you look back, everything is different."[6]

Fred Craddock compares the little things we do in our blank spaces to quarters:

> To give my life for Christ appears glorious. To pour myself out for others . . . to pay the ultimate price of martyrdom—I'll do it. I'm ready, Lord, to go out in a blaze of glory.
>
> We think giving our all to the Lord is like taking a $1,000 bill and laying it on the table—"Here's my life, Lord. I'm giving it all."
>
> But the reality for most of us is that he sends us to the bank and has us cash in the $1,000 for quarters. We go through life putting out 25 cents here and 50 cents there. Listen to the neighbor kid's troubles instead of saying, "Get lost." Go to a committee meeting. Give a cup of water to a shaky old man in a nursing home.
>
> Usually giving our life to Christ isn't glorious. It's done in all those little acts of love, 25 cents at a time. It would be easy to go out in a flash of glory; it's harder to live the Christian life little by little over the long haul.[7]

My prayer is this: "Jesus, help me to be consistent with my 25 cents a day. Teach me that faithfulness counts and to not always look for the big moment but rather for the little places where I can show charity, especially when no one is around and no applause can be heard except for a 'well done' whispered in my spirit."

These 25-cent days fill our blank-space seasons. We're not seeing big exchanges of cash but rather little quarter decisions. As I was studying this passage, I received this text from a church member:

> Pastor Tim, I just had to share with you that I once again took your challenge to read the entire Bible in a year. As usual, I started out strong and then slowly started to fade. After we experienced a flood, friends suggested books and different devotions. I strongly felt a whisper in my heart from God, *Just read my Word.* So I got out my one-year Bible and devoted all my prayer time to reading and journaling over the last eight months. This morning as I finished the entire Bible, I wept. God's Word is so very much alive and a source of hope! The last eight months have truly been a season of restoration, not only of our home, but also my heart. God has used this season as a time of growth and healing. Now I'm thirsty for digging even deeper into His Word and really can't imagine one day going without it.

This precious woman saw what the 25-cents-a-day investment in reading the Bible turned into. What you do every day matters more than what you do once in a great while.

I pastored in Detroit, Michigan, for nearly three

decades. Two of those decades were in a city measuring 2.5 square miles called Highland Park (or HP), which sits in the center of Detroit. This small city is packed with history. The first car in the world was made there. The first paved road was just outside its city limits. The first freeway in the country is there. And the first assembly line to build cars was composed there.

Over the years, however, an ailing Detroit economy, race riots, and a struggling auto industry sent HP sinking into poverty. As businesses closed, porn theaters, prostitution hotels, and adult bookstores filled the vacuum. It was in that district of the city that we started a church.

We bought the flagship porn theater called the Krim Theater on Woodward Avenue and 6 Mile. When we bought the Krim, the owner offered us a second theater for an extra $20,000. I knew I'd have my hands full renovating the nine-hundred-seat Krim, so I passed on the deal. Ishmael!

Hustler magazine came in and took over the second theater and opened up the Déjà Vu Strip Club. They wasted no time putting up a billboard that featured provocative pictures of women to draw in passersby. Every day, I had to look my mistake in the face, just like Abraham had to look Ishmael in the face.

My kids and I launched a 25-cent campaign. When we passed the Déjà Vu on the way to school every morning, we took turns praying the same 25-cent prayer: "God, shrivel up their finances and shut that club down." It doesn't sound like much or seem like a bold move in our eyes, but in God's eyes it was something else. Every prayer was like a sledgehammer smashing into the concrete. And then one day, someone sent me a press release announcing that the Déjà Vu in Highland Park had been shut down.

Don't ever think that the small things you're doing in your blank spaces don't matter. God sees them. Twenty-five cents may not seem like a lot, but those 25-cent days add up to a chunk of change that God can use to bring about real change.

PERSEVERANCE IS ALWAYS PROMOTED

Abraham is known as the father of faith. I believe one of the fruits of a life of faith is perseverance. *Perseverance* is another word for consistency under harsh conditions. It's refusing to give up and quit, regardless of what our emotions are telling us. No one can be persistent by making just one good decision. Perseverance is making the right decision even when we don't feel like it. Successfully navigating the blank spaces involves a lot of perseverance—the way in which faithful people are developed.

To be persistent is to not give up when to do so would be the easiest thing to do. Abraham knew it would have been easier to forget Ishmael, but he chose what was right, not what was easy.

You have persevered when you bought food instead of the shoes or the golf clubs you really wanted, and, yes, they were even on sale. It's when you tithed on your fixed income. It's when you got the family to church when the previous night you were up with the baby for much of the night. That matters! It's taking care of your aging mother and your little kids and realizing it's like being a parent for both. That's perseverance!

A MAN OF PERSEVERANCE

One person who refused to make an easy choice was someone thought to be a failure in his career. Take a look below at this man's track record, and you'll see a life of *perseverance*. In some people's eyes, he was a failure when in reality he was *persistent*.

1818: Mother died when he was nine years old.
1831: Lost his job.
1832: Ran for state legislature—lost.
1833: Borrowed money to begin a business, which went under by the end of the year. Spent several years paying off the debt.
1834: Ran for state legislature again—won.
1835: Sweetheart died, and his heart was broken.
1838: Sought to become speaker of state legislature—defeated.
1843: Failed to achieve party's nomination for Congress.

1846: Ran for Congress and won—went to Washington, DC, and did a good job.

1849: Applied to become commissioner of the General Land Office—rejected.

1854: Sought seat in the United States Senate— withdrew after deadlocked process.

1856: Name put into nomination for vice president at his party's national convention—not elected.

1858: Candidate for US Senate—did not take the seat.

1860: Elected president of the United States—reelected in 1864.[8]

Who was this man? Abraham Lincoln—a man who persevered when each failure and setback were screaming at him to give up.

Another word for perseverance is *faithfulness*. God rewards faithfulness, and it's what He commends in heaven: "Well done, good and faithful servant!" (Matthew 25:23 NIV). God recognized Abraham as being faithful, even though his faithfulness was demonstrated through managing his mistake.

YOUR GREATEST CHAPTER COMES SUDDENLY

Chapter 17 was Abraham's dream chapter.

Seemingly out of nowhere, God gave Abraham the greatest chapter of his life. It happened with no warning. Abraham wasn't ministering, preaching, writing books, recording podcasts. He wasn't doing famous things, but rather faithful things. The greatest chapter came not because he was doing anything great in man's eyes but because he was doing something great in God's eyes.

The faithful Christian life is not an incline, but a flatline followed by a sudden spike. It flatlined for Abraham for thirteen years and then suddenly—the greatest chapter of his life. God is able to do things suddenly.

You may think your blank spaces are redundant, monotonous, boring, and uneventful, but they are actually a prelude to the greatest season of your life. Don't stop and abort in that season. This is where God is making faithful men and women. All those 25-cent decisions add up.

Little things matter, so don't grow weary. Perseverance is always promoted, so don't give up. Your greatest chapter comes suddenly, so get ready.

DISCUSSION QUESTIONS

1. Name one of the "little hinges"—a daily routine—you may have minimized. Share something about how your faithfulness to that seemingly small responsibility might help you in the future.
2. As you reflect on your life, have you ever quit something because you thought it was "boring" or "meaningless"? Do you wish you would have stuck it out?
3. What qualities can you pray for to cultivate the kind of faithfulness Abraham demonstrated?

CHAPTER 4

MAKING THE MOST OF OUR WORST DAYS WITH PETER

The gospel is this: We are more sinful and flawed
in ourselves than we ever dared believe, yet at
the same time we are more loved and accepted
in Jesus Christ than we ever dared hope.

Tim Keller, *The Meaning of Marriage*

When you have little ones, you get to read children's books. And when you have a lot of children, you get to read a lot of them. C. S. Lewis wrote this about children's books: "No book is really worth reading at the age of ten which is not equally (and often far more) worth reading at the age of fifty. . . . The only imaginative works we ought to grow out of are those which it would have been better not to have read at all."[1]

Many of the books I've read to my young children have impacted me, and when that happens, I know it's a good children's book. One of those fun books that cross the age barrier is Judith Viorst's *Alexander and the Terrible, Horrible, No Good, Very Bad Day*. Alexander describes his day from the moment he wakes up to the time he goes to bed. Every moment seems to be glorious for everyone else but a train wreck for him.

> I went to sleep with gum in my mouth and now there's gum in my hair, when I got out of bed this morning I tripped on the skateboard and by mistake I dropped my sweater in the sink while the water was running and I could tell it was going to be a terrible, horrible, no good, very bad day. . . . I think I'll move to Australia.[2]

The story is funny because it contains truth and experiences we can all relate to. Our lives would be better if only we could go somewhere else. For Alexander, the mindset is that it must be better in Australia.

Alexander finds it hard to believe that Australians have bad days. Some of us find it just as hard to believe that Christians can have bad days too. God never promises that once you become a Christian, every day will be perfect. We'll have some good days—what I refer to as "Peter days"—but we'll have bad days too, or what we might call "Satan days."

A BRAND-NEW NAME

If there is one Bible character we see at their worst and at their best, it is the apostle Peter. The person we hear from most often among the disciples is the most flawed. In one of Peter's encounters with Jesus, we see Peter at his worst and at his best, but what makes the account both sad and hilarious is how fast it happens. It goes from first to worst so fast.

In Matthew 16, Jesus asked the disciples a monumental question:

> "Who do people say that the Son of Man is?" And [His disciples] said, "Some say John the Baptist; and others, Elijah; and still others, Jeremiah, or one of the other prophets." He said to them, "But who do you yourselves say that I am?" (Matthew 16:13–15)

Here's where we see Peter shine:

> Simon Peter answered, "You are the Christ, the Son of the living God." And Jesus said to him, "Blessed are you, Simon Barjona, because flesh and blood did not reveal this to you, but My Father who is in heaven. And I also say to you that you are Peter, and upon this rock I will build My church; and the gates of Hades will not over-power it." (Matthew 16:16–18)

Wow! Jesus changed Peter's name because Peter had his own revelation of who Jesus is. It didn't happen to the other disciples, but it happened to Peter. This was a good moment for Peter.

Our story isn't over though. On the heels of a new revelation, which Jesus said came directly from the Father in heaven, Peter seems to get a little cocky and believe his own press clippings. Peter got the answer right to "Who do people say that I am?" He gets the next part totally wrong:

> From that time Jesus began to point out to His disciples that it was necessary for Him to go to Jerusalem and to suffer many things from the elders, chief priests, and scribes, and to be killed, and to be raised up on the third day. And yet Peter took Him aside and began to rebuke Him, saying, "God forbid it, Lord! This shall never happen to You!" But He turned and said to Peter, "Get behind Me, Satan! You are a stumbling block to Me; for you are not setting your mind on God's purposes, but men's." (Matthew 16:21–23)

Peter got another name change here. And what a change it was! The disciple went from Peter to Satan in just five verses.

Have you ever felt like that? Like you just got it right, but before you can lift the trophy, you got it really wrong. Welcome to the life of the apostle Peter.

It is through Peter that we see the unique way God

works with failure. It's part of God's process to utilize us, even when we fail. It's when God invites you to come in after you've utterly failed. It's when God chooses to call your name when your name is mud. It's when God asks you to speak even after knowing that the last time you spoke didn't go very well. This is not God's lesson on getting back on the horse; it's a lesson on why God would let us use His horse in the first place.

That is the life of Peter.

WHOSE WORDS ARE YOU SPEAKING?

Peter goes through a few name changes in Scripture, so let me give a quick review. Prior to Matthew 16, Peter was called Simon. Then Peter hit a home run with his revelation of who Jesus is, and Jesus changed his name from Simon to Peter. And then the next moment, Peter earned his worst name yet—Satan.

We can relate to the circumstances around each of Peter's names. We all live Simon days—those common, ordinary days when life happens. Then, unexpectedly, we get that rare Peter moment of revelation. We do or experience something monumental. God promotes us at our job, on our campus, or in the eyes of our family. We move from Simon days to Peter days. Peter days feel great. But just as suddenly as a Peter day happens, we find ourselves living a Satan day.

Peter's life is our life. And that life is part of the process that God uses. It's a process to remind us that God's fingerprints are all over any achievement we make.

Now, Peter was the one who spoke the revelation that earned him his "claim to fame" name, but the revelation itself came from the Father. It was Peter's mouth but God's content. I have this funny feeling that Peter chose to forget that. Or perhaps he had selective hearing. I think he heard, "You are blessed, Simon," and then nothing until Jesus said, "I say to you that you are Peter . . . and upon this rock I will build my church" (Matthew 16:18 NLT). He had to have missed, "My Father in heaven has revealed this to you. You did not learn this from any human being" (16:17 NLT). Peter was so focused on "blessed" and "upon this rock" that he forgot the source of his revelation. Perhaps that was what led him to offer such a hasty answer in the next exchange.

When Jesus talked for the first time to the disciples about the cross, it was for them to digest and ponder, not to give Him their opinion or commentary. If Peter had fully understood that his brilliance in the previous exchange was due to God's revelation, not his own wisdom, he might have said, "Father, do you have anything else you want me to say?" If he had done that, he would have heard, "Nothing," because nothing was needed as Jesus shared about His cross.

Peter didn't pray, but Peter did speak. And this time when he spoke, his words were not God's but his own—with the result that he was called Satan. Such harsh words for the man who had a revelation! They had to be harsh because only Satan would want to stop Jesus from going to the cross. Jesus was speaking not just to Peter but to the enemy that was using Peter. Just as the Father used Peter's mouth for revelation, the father of lies was using his mouth for abomination.

A good day became a great day, and then a great day became a horrible day.

SATAN DAYS

We have this strange theology that God tolerates us on Simon days and really likes us on our great Peter days, but when a Satan day comes—canceled! Nothing could be further from the truth. Your worst days don't make you any less accepted by God.

That is hard to fathom. We are so bent toward performance because performance promotion is ingrained in all we do—from our jobs to our sports to our relationships. It's hard to fathom that the prodigal son covered in mud in a pigpen never stopped being a son and never stopped being loved by his father—countercultural to our way of thinking. To be loved in the midst of a poor performance seems unthinkable. It doesn't register.

I struggled with this concept until one morning a few years ago as I rode the NYC subway. When no seat is available on the train, I listen to a podcast. When I do find a seat, I read a book. That morning, I found an open seat, so it was a book-reading morning. I was reading *The Furious Longing of God* by Brennan Manning, an author who has had a profound effect on my life. His words changed the way I think about my many Satan days:

> The challenge, so keenly put in the New Testament—"Who do you say that I am?"—is addressed to each of us. Who is the Jesus of your own making? Describe the Christ that you have personally encountered on the grounds of your own self?
>
> For His love is never, never, never based on our performance, never conditioned by our moods—of elation or depression. The furious love of God knows no shadow of alteration or change. It is always reliable. And always tender. . . .
>
> The revolutionary thinking that God loves me as I am and not as I should be requires radical rethinking and profound emotional readjustment. . . .
>
> Two important corollaries flow from this life-changing revolution. First, if we continue to picture God as a small-minded bookkeeper, a niggling customs officer rifling through our moral suitcase, as a policeman with a club who is going to bat us over the head every time we stumble and fall, or as a whimsical, capricious, and cantankerous thief who delights in raining on our parade and stealing our joy, we flatly deny what

John writes in his first letter (4:16)—"God is love." In human beings, love is a quality, a high-prized virtue; in God, love is his identity. . . .

How is it then that we've come to imagine that Christianity consists primarily in what we do for God? How has this come to be the good news of Jesus? Is the kingdom that he proclaimed to be nothing more than a community of men and women who go to church on Sunday, take an annual spiritual retreat, read their Bibles every now and then, vigorously oppose abortion, don't watch x-rated movies, never use vulgar language, smile a lot, hold doors open for people, root for the favorite team, and get along with everybody? Is that why Jesus went through the bleak and bloody horror of Calvary? Is that why he emerged in shattering glory from the tomb? Is that why he poured out his Holy Spirit on the church? To make nicer men and women with better morals? . . .

Our religion never begins with what we do for God. It always starts with what God has done for us, the great and wondrous things that God dreamed of and achieved for us in Christ Jesus.[3]

And then I grabbed a second Brennan Manning book I had with me and came across these words:

If Jesus sat at your dining-room table tonight with full knowledge of everything you are and are not; if he laid out your whole life-story, with the hidden agenda and the dark desires unknown even to yourself, it would still be impossible to be saddened in his presence.[4]

I started to tear up around the Rockefeller Center stop. The thought of Jesus sitting at my dinner table and knowing every dark place in me and the impossibility of my being sad in His presence, fully knowing that He knows, was powerful. He knows everything about me. What makes Jesus amazing is that He absolutely knows you and me and every evil and wicked thought, and He not only accepts us but *furiously loves us*. Even on Satan days.

Peter's experience after his Satan day was proof of Jesus' unwavering love and provides insight into God's process. My response to Peter would have been to take him to a private place and say, "Peter, now think about what you just said. We don't say those things to Jesus when He is speaking about the cross. I want you to really think hard about why Jesus called you Satan. I'll be back, and then we can discuss it." That's me, but that's not Jesus.

What does Jesus do? He does what only Jesus would do. "Six days later, Jesus took with Him Peter and James, and his brother John, and led them up on a high mountain by themselves" (Matthew 17:1).

While we were convinced Peter would get a time-out, he got an invitation.

You don't invite Satan to the Mount of Transfiguration, but that's what Jesus did.

There are relatively few moments when Jesus' deity

leaks out and He allows people to see more heaven on Him than humanity. The Mount of Transfiguration was one of those times when the God-Man had the God part in bold letters. What makes this an incredible act of grace on the Master's part was everything that Peter would witness and overhear on this mountain: "He was transfigured before them; and His face shone like the sun, and His garments became as white as light. And behold, Moses and Elijah appeared to them, talking with Him" (Matthew 17:2–3).

This scene should be enough to overwhelm us with the mercy of Jesus. But what makes this even more amazing is the topic of conversation among Moses, Elijah, and Jesus: "They were speaking of his death at Jerusalem, to be carried out in accordance with God's plan" (Luke 9:31 TLB). Did you get that? They were speaking about the cross—the very topic Peter got an F in!

When we have done our worst and have been our worst, God deems it necessary to not sit us in a corner, but rather to invite us to a place where we feel we have no business going to. And just as Peter's revelation was from the Father, so was his invitation. Peter didn't earn or originate either. Peter's story illustrates what the apostle Paul emphatically wrote: "What are you so puffed up about? What do you have that God hasn't given you? And if all you have is from God, why act as though you are so great, and as though you have accomplished something on your own?" (1 Corinthians 4:7 TLB).

What makes grace so amazing is that our behavior

does not dictate God's behavior. He cannot not be who He is based on who you are. Your actions, whether good or bad, don't control His character. In another of his letters, Paul reminds us, "If we are unfaithful, he remains faithful, for he cannot deny who he is" (2 Timothy 2:13 NLT). God can't be anything less than who He is. Your unfaithfulness doesn't change God's faithfulness.

We all have relationships that are performance based: I'll be good to you if you're good to me. I'll give to you if you give to me. I'll love you if you love me. But who can actually say, "Your worst days toward me don't change how I feel about you"? Your bad days, your Satan days, do not change how God feels about you.

As the story goes, Thomas Edison was hard at work on an invention that would change the world. It's something we benefit from every day—the light bulb. Jim Newton, who became a member of Edison's household in the years before Edison's death, said that it took a team of people twenty-four hours straight to produce just one bulb.

Newton related that when Edison was finished with one light bulb, he gave it to a young boy, who nervously carried it up the stairs: "Step by step, he cautiously watched his hands, obviously frightened of dropping such a priceless piece of work. But the boy was concentrating so hard on making sure the bulb didn't slip from his hands that he forgot to watch his feet. He tripped at the top of the stairs and dropped the bulb and it shattered."

It took the entire team of men another twenty-four

hours to make the second light bulb. Finally, tired and ready for a break, Edison was ready to have his bulb carried up the stairs. Guess who got the invitation again?

Edison gave it to the same young boy who had dropped the first one. This time the light bulb made it to the top of the stairs.[5]

When what you've worked so hard on—something that will change the world—is dropped by a kid and destroyed in a moment, who has the audacity to give that kid a second chance with something that revolutionary? Jesus had a light bulb, and Jesus had a clumsy kid. The light bulb was to become the church, and the kid's name was Peter. His "stair drop" would be denying Jesus three times at Jesus' most crucial moment of His life. And after the resurrection, Jesus found Peter and was ready to give him the light bulb again.

God is amazing because He doesn't just forgive us after failure; He trusts us after failure. King David wrote, "If you, GOD, kept records on wrongdoings, who would stand a chance? As it turns out, forgiveness is your habit, and that's why you're worshiped" (Psalm 130:3–4 MSG).

Abraham Lincoln is reported to have said, "My great concern is not whether you have failed, but whether you are content with your failure."[6] Jesus was making sure Peter was not content with failure and thinking about moving to "Australia."

Failure is part of life and everyone fails. Getting up from failure is where the numbers thin out. Failure isn't final until we quit. Jesus would not let Peter quit.

We serve an incredible God—a God who stands closest when we blow it the worst. Though my actions can be unpredictable, I am thankful for a God who is very predictable. Because I have a lot more Satan days than Peter days, I need the assurance that He is closest when I am at my worst.

God brought Peter into one of those moments in Jesus' time on earth when His divinity leaked through His humanity. Jesus didn't bring Peter the revelation guy; He brought Peter the "Get behind me, Satan" guy. Part of God's process is inviting us, speaking to us, and using us when we're at our worst. God uses us in horrible times to remind us that He is always behind everything. It's one of His processes to keep us close during our Satan days when we feel unworthy. That's when God invites us to a mountain to see heaven opened. And in those times, we fight unworthiness and the feeling that we are the last people who should be in God's presence. This is God's way of reminding us of His love, His work, and His grace. The words of the psalmist David fit well here: "He Himself knows our form; He is mindful that we are nothing but dust" (Psalm 103:14).

FROM DENIER TO CHURCH LAUNCHER

Have you ever heard the saying, "You are not defined by your past but prepared by your past"?[7] If one's past refers to their failures, Peter was really prepared for his future.

Then the unimaginable took place. God had plans for the denier. After Jesus' resurrection, He sent the apostles to an upper room in Jerusalem to prepare for the coming of the Holy Spirit and the launching of the church. If there was one city Peter did *not* want to be in, it was Jerusalem—the scene of Peter's denial. While he was there, fire from heaven fell upon the 120. And it was now time to preach to the thousands gathered in Jerusalem and to launch the first church.

Who do you think had the honor of preaching the very first sermon in church history? You guessed it! The kid who dropped the light bulb. God chose the denier, Peter. The man who denied Jesus in Jerusalem weeks earlier to a few people in a courtyard would now proclaim Him in Jerusalem to thousands. That day, three thousand people came to Christ, and the church was started.

UNIMAGINABLE OPPORTUNITIES

Devotional writer Oswald Chambers wrote, "Leave the broken, irreversible past in [God's] hands, and step out into the invincible future with Him."[8] I think those who fail miserably subsequently receive unimaginable opportunities from God and therefore have a great appreciation for His grace. When God invites us into His story, despite our failures, onlookers may gawk even as we are overcome by our experiences of grace. Augustine offers a powerful reminder to us Peters: "[Grace] is given not because we have done good works, but in order that we may have power to do them."[9]

> Help, God —I've hit rock bottom!
>   Master, hear my cry for help!
> Listen hard! Open your ears!
>   Listen to my cries for mercy.
>
> If you, God, kept records on wrongdoings,
>   who would stand a chance?
> As it turns out, forgiveness is your habit,
>   and that's why you're worshiped.
>   (Psalm 130:1–4 MSG)

DISCUSSION QUESTIONS

1. Great failings seem to have a way of happening on the way to church. Can you remember a time when you were heading to worship and you failed with your spouse, your children, your attitude? How did you go from failure to worship?

2. Has God used you in a surprising way in a conversation to share the gospel, though you felt you weren't worthy to be used in such a way? Why did you feel that way?

3. "Australia" for us usually means seclusion—the other side of the world, a place where no one knows us. When you find yourself having a "Satan day" with your children, your coworker, or your spouse, don't retreat into a corner; rather, ask God for His amazing invitation to go up higher. What is the best way to snap out of an "Australia" moment?

CHAPTER 5

APPRECIATING COMMUNITY WITH PAUL

If you want to go fast, go alone.
If you want to go far, go together.
African proverb

For any pastor of a church, there's one relationship that is always important—the one with your sound opera-tor. This relationship can make or break a Sunday service. A lot is riding on these tech folks. I see them as the offen-sive linemen for NFL quarterbacks. It doesn't matter how well they can throw—if the defense always sacks them, they never get the chance to make the play. Sound oper-ators are the offensive line. If they don't get it right, then I can't be right.

I count every sound operator among my friends in

every city in which I've pastored. I even become friends with the sound guys in the cities I visit and speak in because, in my mind, my relationship with them there is even more crucial. I have one shot to get it right.

It seems like wherever I am, there comes a moment right after I've said the final "amen" that I realize I forgot to say something important, so I have to tell the sound operators to turn the microphone back on. That's when I need them to be especially alert.

When I read Paul's letter to the Romans, I realized I was in good company. He had a "turn the microphone back on" moment in this epistle. In chapter 15, Paul offered a closing prayer and concluded by saying, "Now the God of peace be with you all. Amen" (Romans 15:33).

When I hear "amen," I hear, "We are done." "Meeting over." "Time to go home." Even "Time to eat." I imagine Paul's original audience stood up and stretched their legs, ready to head home. But then Paul started speaking again. It's almost like he stopped everyone and said, "Wait, wait, wait. I forgot something. Please turn my microphone back on."

And what he said ends up being one of the most amazing and overlooked passages in the New Testament. In the twenty-seven verses between his first amen in Romans 15:33 and his second amen in Romans 16:27, Paul mentions thirty-three names. These weren't just any old people, but thirty-three people who had helped him in ministry. Some of the little vignettes around these thirty-three names are priceless. Paul singled out four women in the first seven names. Phoebe, the first name mentioned, was a business-woman who delivered the letter of Romans to this church. He thanked a special ministry couple, Prisca and Aquila, who "risked their own necks for my life" (Romans 16:4). He mentioned Mary, a hard worker. He talked about others who were outstanding Christians and fellow cellmates. And those were just a few of the thirty-three people he mentioned.

Paul used his "turn the microphone back on" moment to acknowledge that there was no way he could do this kingdom work without those thirty-three people.

WHERE RECOGNITION IS DUE

There will never be an NCAA basketball coach like the Wizard of Westwood. I'm speaking, of course, of UCLA's John Wooden. This famous coach won ten National Championships in twelve years. You heard it right—*ten!* He had a winning percentage of over .800. In one of his books, *A Game Plan for Life*, Wooden wrote, "When one of my players scored, he knew he was supposed to point to the teammate who had passed him the ball or made the block that allowed that basket to happen. It wasn't about deflecting praise, but about sharing it with everyone who was working hard as a part of the team."[1] This is genius and countercultural in today's sports arena. Today everyone thumps their chest and the team has to follow them around the court and the field as they carry on without giving any recognition to anyone who helped them get through an offensive line or get to the hoop to throw one down.

When was the last time you saw a defensive end sack a quarterback and then turn around and point to every defensive lineman who made the hole that opened the way for him? Never! It just doesn't happen. That linebacker will stand in the middle of the field as if his talent alone gave him that moment and the momentum to get through eleven players on his own. If those players played for John Wooden, I don't think they would have been there for long.

The apostle Paul took a page out of Coach Wooden's notebook. He wrapped up Romans by pointing to thirty-three people who had given him the ball, opened the line, and gotten him into the end zone. Romans 16 pointed fingers instead of thumping chests. Paul was acknowledging he couldn't be who he was without all those people.

Part of Paul's journey was learning the value of people. This is an imperative part of the process. His life and ministry couldn't have flourished without those people cheering him on. And they weren't the only ones. There were more than the thirty-three names found in Romans 16. At Paul's conversion, there was Ananias, who would be the first to encounter the ex-murderer and terrorist and pray for him (Acts 9). There was Barnabas, famous for being an encourager, who believed in Paul's calling long before the leadership of the first church did and who invited him to help in a revival (Acts 11). There was the unnamed nephew in Acts who got wind of a plot to kill Uncle Paul, informed him, and ended up saving Paul's life (Acts 23).

Paul knew the truth of these words written by newspaper columnist George Matthew Adams: "There is no such thing as a 'self-made' man. We are made up of thousands of others. Everyone who has ever done a kind deed for us, or spoken one word of encouragement to us, has entered into the make-up of our character and of our thoughts, as well as our successes."[2] There really *is* no such thing as a self-made man.

The Christian life isn't meant to be lived alone. Only weak people think they are strong enough to do the Christian life by themselves. All of us should occasionally put together a list of names, making sure we take time to appreciate the people who are doing life with us, because if we don't appreciate someone, we depreciate them.

Honestly, we will never make it through our story without the right people in our lives. And the need for people intensifies as we get older. By the time Paul wrote Romans, he had been a Christian for more than two decades. We older believers can use the reminder that we need people for every step along our Christian journey.

Nowhere is this principle better illustrated than in the story of the Old Testament character David and his "mighty men." Anyone who hears the name David instantly associates his name with a giant with whom he engaged in one of the most famous battles of the Bible—the David and Goliath story. David's first giant story we know, but it wasn't his only giant story.

The last giant faced is another Philistine, and the shepherd isn't a young man anymore. He is an old king. The story is told in 2 Samuel 21. It's a reminder of what to do when rocks won't work.

> Now when the Philistines were at war with Israel again, David went down, and his servants with him; and when they fought against the Philistines, David became weary. Then Ishbi-benob, who was among the descendants of the giant, the weight of whose spear was three hundred shekels of bronze in weight, had strapped on a new sword, and he intended to kill David. (2 Samuel 21:15–16)

So how did David win? He needed another weapon. Not a rock, but a friend, a brother, a mighty man of God. The new rock was Abishai. David learned the Romans 16 lesson on the battlefield at a crucial time. The older we become, the more we need one another, which was proven true by one of the greatest individuals of faith who ever lived and perhaps the greatest Old Testament king.

While God has us on our personal journey, we can build our Abishai base. The name Abishai in Hebrew means "father of a gift." We must find the gifts in relationships. I've also learned that the more we grow in God, the bigger the giants become. The giants may not be as frequent as they used to be, but they surely got a lot taller and tougher. The closer we get to the realization of our dream, the greater the chance that significant giants will rise up and old rocks won't work. We will need the gift of friendships we've collected on our journey.

Older and wiser David did not need a sling but a church family to take out this giant. Paul needed a community of thirty-three. David needed a mighty man—Abishai. It goes without saying, but I'll say it anyway: If King David and the apostle Paul needed help, we need help as well.

IMMOVABLE IN NUMBERS

There is a particular structure that soars three hundred feet into the sky—almost the length of a football field. But what makes this structure an anomaly is that its roots only go down five feet into the ground. It's true. What structure is this? It's the mighty redwood tree.

Redwood trees break the rules. Given their height, we'd expect them to have a deeper root system. How do they stay upright? They never grow alone. As they grow high, their roots intertwine with the trees around them below the surface, and that's what keeps them from blowing over and uprooting in a storm. To try to blow one over means we are really fighting against all of them. Redwoods always grow together in numbers. It's what makes them immovable.

Paul needed a root system, and so do we. Root systems

help us in three ways: (1) we get smarter, (2) we get healthier, and (3) we get stronger.

SMARTER TOGETHER

Those who connect with others get smarter. The writer of Proverbs says, "One who walks with wise people will be wise" (Proverbs 13:20). I love what C. S. Lewis said: "The next best thing to being wise oneself is to live in a circle of those who are."[3] One of my dear friends used to say, "Show me your friends, and I will show you your future."[4] When we isolate, we become dumber.

Since the Bible tells us that we gain wisdom from many good counselors (see Proverbs 15:22), how do we get wise if we don't have many good counselors around us? "In an abundance of counselors there is victory" (Proverbs 11:14) and "One who walks with wise people will be wise" (Proverbs 13:20) are even more profound because of who said these things.

Solomon was the writer of Proverbs—a man known for his wisdom. He was called the wisest man who ever lived. You would think the wisest man who ever lived wouldn't need anyone to give him counsel. But the opposite is true. Solomon said he needed counselors and wise voices in his journey. How many people have processed with the worst three counselors we get when we're all alone: me, myself, and I?

When I was planting my first church in Detroit, Michigan, I sat in David Wilkerson's apartment in midtown

Manhattan and asked him for any counsel he could give me. I still live by his words: "Find grayheads to be around. You need wise people in your life."

What we call finding grayheads is "processing up." We give our children, friends, and coworkers a negative example when we refuse to process up with our elders when we need wisdom and help in making decisions. And think about this: "Up" means people who have more maturity and more of life's journey under their belts than we do.

They are the "grayheads" who have navigated through pain to success in life. The Contemporary English Version paraphrases Proverbs 13:20 like this: "Wise friends make you wise, but you hurt yourself by going around with fools." We must strive to have a circle of people around us who are further down the road than we are and are doing what we want to be doing.

This may confuse some people, but it's important to say, "My best friend's advice does not count when I'm making a big decision." They are too biased. Rather than going horizontal on big decisions, we need to process *up*. We need bigger voices and older voices. Our decisions matter for our lives and for those who come after us.

Moments after the apostle Paul's conversion (Acts 9), God connected the new convert with a grayhead named Ananias, who some think was a prophet in the early church. God knew the person Paul would need to lead him into his future. Ananias would lay hands on Paul so he would see clearly again. That's exactly what those gray-heads do. They help us see clearly—and when we see more clearly, we are smarter.

HEALTHIER TOGETHER

The team of "the thirty-three" also gets us healthier. We often forget that our *spiritual* healing is connected to godly people.

James 5:16 is an often-misquoted New Testament verse. Here's the translation many people use: "The effectual fervent prayer of a righteous man availeth much" (KJV). This was the way I quoted that verse as I was growing up. And then I discovered that these ten words make up the last part of the verse. The first part reads as follows: "Confess your faults one to another, and pray one for another, that ye may be healed." James was saying that when we confess our faults or struggles to someone, we're doing it *for healing.*

But where does the healing come from? It comes from the person who knows how to pray and get ahold of God for you. In effect, James was saying, "Are you fighting a giant? Don't talk to your girlfriend, your golfing buddy, your fantasy football friend, or your neighbor. You need to find someone who can knock out a giant for you in prayer. You need to find your thirty-three and get them praying for you. Because when you do, your healing begins."

This is how the verse goes when it all comes together: "Confess your faults one to another, and pray one for another, that ye may be healed. The effectual fervent prayer of a righteous man availeth much" (James 5:16 KJV).

Over the years of my ministry life, I found myself in some toxic situations that were unhealthy for my soul. I did not have the energy or the expertise to get myself free from the funk that was clouding my thinking and vision. I needed help, and I needed it fast. God gave me a gift—like Abishai was for David and the thirty-three were for Paul—by providing prayer warriors to get me through. Righteous people who made me a prayer priority. I grew up in the church, where we'd hear this common phrase: "Son, you got to pray through." But how do you pray through when you can't see through to the next day? That's where I was spiritually. Hallelujah, God sends help! I am a witness that it was the prayers of others who prayed me back to health.

STRONGER TOGETHER

Finally, we need a root system of relationships to make us stronger. The Bible says that one will put a thousand to flight but two can put ten thousand to flight (see Deuteronomy 32:30). When we're intertwined with the right people, it makes us ten times better than being all by ourselves.

People today always seem to be fighting over what is the greatest "man movie" of all time. Seniors go with *The Godfather*. Boomers say *Braveheart*. Some younger guys say *300*. Gen Zers point to the Marvel movies. But everyone knows it's *Gladiator*. This movie, set in second-century Rome, tells the story of how a general became a slave and a gladiator who defied an emperor. Russell Crowe plays Maximus the gladiator. When Maximus is in the Colosseum, he tells the other gladiators, "Whatever comes out of these gates, we've got a better chance of survival if we work together. Do you understand? If we stay together we survive."[5] Maximus knew this to be true because that's how his Roman soldiers would fight. They would lock arms and connect shields. They were saying, *You may be able to beat me when I am alone, but I'm not alone.*

Paul seems to be reminding us of this principle in Ephesians 6, where he talks about spiritual warfare. This chapter has an interesting contrast. Paul declared that we don't fight "flesh and blood" but "powers of darkness." He was speaking about our fight with Satan and was identifying an important contrast:

> Finally, my brethren, be strong in the Lord and in the power of His might. Put on the whole armor of God, that you may be able to stand against the wiles of the devil. For we do not wrestle against flesh and blood, but against principalities, against powers, against the rulers of the darkness of this age, against spiritual hosts of wickedness in the heavenly places. Therefore take up the whole armor of God, that you may be able to withstand in the evil day, and having done all, to stand. (Ephesians 6:10–13 NKJV)

The contrast Paul snuck into this passage was the difference between a wrestler and a soldier.

Paul wrote in verse 12, "We do not wrestle," and then in the next verse he wrote, "Take up the whole armor of God." Paul unveiled a most important tool for fighting the enemy. He was giving us redwood advice. Second-century wrestlers fought alone. They would oil their bodies and fight to the death. And Paul said, "We do *not* wrestle." We don't fight that way as Christians. Then came Paul's transition to "take up the whole armor of God." We are not wrestlers, but rather soldiers.

We don't fight alone but with our thirty-three, with our redwoods. We don't fight alone as Christians because we are an army, not a solo act.

SHARE THE WORK, SHARE THE WEALTH

In track, there are two races that go the same distance—the first is a solo race, and the second has four participants. The first is the 400-meter dash; the second is the 4 x 400-meter relay. In the relay, four runners each complete one 400-meter lap.

The men's outdoor world record for the relay is 2:54.29. The men's world record for the mile (approximately 1,600 meters) is 3:43.13. Note that it takes nearly a minute longer to run by yourself, which means if we run against a relay the same distance, we will come in last every single time.

Regardless of how fast we start, we don't have the legs to finish.

I would rather run this race knowing my thirty-three were waiting for me to pass them the baton because their fresh legs can go farther and faster.

All along our journey, God connects us with His people, many of whom seem to be people who go to your church. I believe that somewhere in that group are your thirty-three. And those are the ones who make you stronger for the fight. As the wise king Solomon wrote, "It's better to have a partner than go it alone. Share the work, share the wealth. And if one falls down, the other helps, but if there's no one to help, tough! Two in a bed warm each other. Alone, you shiver all night. By yourself you're unprotected. With a friend you can face the worst. Can you round up a third? A three-stranded rope isn't easily snapped" (Ecclesiastes 4:9–12 MSG).

I once heard it said, "When Satan wants to mess with you, he sends the wrong people; when God wants to bless you, he sends the right people."

Let's get the right people in our lives and be blessed.

DISCUSSION QUESTIONS

1. Consider something you learned from a seasoned leader in your journey that you never could have learned alone. How has that lesson helped you overcome obstacles in your life?

2. Are you in the habit of doing what Paul did—pausing to thank your thirty-three? Share some ways you can thank people for their help in getting you to where you are today.

3. Consider some new habits you could adopt as you end conversations with people. Share one or two ideas about what you can do to support people you care about before you leave or end a call.

CHAPTER 6

FINDING YOUR PEOPLE AND PURPOSE WITH RAHAB

No Christian is an only child.
Eugene H. Peterson, *A Long Obedience
in the Same Direction*

I ministered to prostitutes for almost three decades in Detroit. It was not something I was called to do but *had* to do because of the location of our church. I had no choice but to have our people minister to these precious men and women who had lost their way.

I knew one young woman who hated what she had become so much so that she found herself washing her skin until she bled. She was trying to scrub her past off her body. I knew a young woman whose addiction was so overpowering that she was turning tricks with a full leg cast on, the result of a pimp breaking her leg with a 5-iron golf club. The lifestyle of these men and women strips them of their identity and gives them very little hope of recovering it.

For many years, our church in Detroit had a 6:00 a.m. prayer meeting Monday through Friday. Each morning, I pulled up to meet the parishioners coming to pray, and I'd also meet some of the prostitutes ending their night shift. I remember one young woman who greeted me as I entered the church. When I asked what her name was, she said, "Mocha." Recognizing that as a street name, I asked her what name she was given at birth. "Cynthia," she answered. She looked as if she had not heard that name for many years. Her voice seemed to change as she thought back to being a little girl. It seemed as if she was trying to go back and recover her innocence. She was hearing her God-given name on the very streets that had taken that part of her identity from her. I hoped that by recalling her true name, it would awaken something in her soul and remind her that she is much more than her present self. I hoped she would walk with me through the doors into a prayer meeting, where she would find a group of people who could point her to the way out of her dark past and into her God-blessed future. I wanted Mocha to become Cynthia that morning, and I wanted similar transformation for every one of those young women in front of our church.

Cynthia never did take those three steps into that

prayer meeting, though others did. But there was a prostitute in the Bible who did take steps toward God and the new life He offers—and she made history.

RISKING IT ALL

No one displays a way out of a past like the prostitute Rahab, whom we meet in the book of Joshua. Her story is epic.

Joshua 2 tells of a prostitute named Rahab who lived in the city of Jericho. One day, she heard a knock on her door. She probably thought, *Well, business as usual.* It was a normal thing for men to come to her door. But this day, the men were not normal. They were not there to escort her deeper into her darkness; they were there to lead her into an amazing future.

The two men who knocked on her door were Israelite spies sent by General Joshua to spy out the land. These spies knew about God's power to rescue people from slavery because they were among those delivered from four hundred years of bondage to the Egyptians. And these two men knew about walking into their future and destiny, because Jericho would be the first obstacle in the way of their destination—the promised land.

I wonder if Rahab saw that these men were different from the men she knew in Jericho. Maybe she saw something in their eyes or heard it in their voices. I think she had to know that something was different about these two visitors. If she didn't at first, she would soon, because shortly after she invited them into her home, she received a message from the king of Jericho inquiring if she had any information about two Israelite spies.

It would have been easy for her to tell the king the truth. She might have even received a reward for ratting on these two guys. But instead she lied. "Yes, the men came to me. . . . I do not know where the men went," Rahab said to the king's messenger, when in fact she had hidden the two spies on her rooftop (Joshua 2:4–5).

Rahab saw her future in these two men, and she was willing to risk the death penalty by housing them just so she could discover God's future for her. She was rewarded for her choice with life—and a new destiny.

WALLS FALL DOWN

I'm not surprised that God used the two spies to rescue a prostitute from her predicament and get her moving toward her epic future. The spies volunteered for the dangerous mission because they saw what the future for Israel could be. They were willing to risk their lives on a recon mission because they knew a big wall—the one encircling Jericho—was standing between them and their future.

The prostitute Rahab was facing a wall of her own—not a literal wall, but a wall that was holding her back just as effectively as if it had been made of brick and mortar. Her wall was her sins and her sordid past.

After Rahab lied to the king's messengers, she returned to the rooftop where she had hidden the spies underneath stalks of flax and revealed her motive for helping the men:

> "I know that the LORD has given you the land, and that the terror of you has fallen on us, and that all the inhabitants of the land have despaired because of you. For we have heard how the LORD dried up the water of the Red Sea before you when you came out of Egypt, and what you did to the two kings of the Amorites who were beyond the Jordan, to Sihon and Og, whom you utterly destroyed. When we heard these reports, our hearts melted and no courage remained in anyone any longer because of you; for the LORD your God, He is God in heaven above and on earth below." (Joshua 2:8–11)

Remember, not a sword had been lifted against Jericho yet. But the people of Jericho were living in fear of the Israelites because of a forty-year-old story swirling around the city, being told over and over again. It was a miracle story that was so big that by the time it got to Jericho, people probably thought it was exaggerated. The story was simple: the God of the Israelites is so big that He divided the Red Sea for them after setting them free from Egypt. Seriously? A sea divided?

The Red Sea miracle was fighting for the Israelites in

Jericho long before they reached Jericho. Israel's enemies had simply *heard* about the miracle of the Red Sea crossing and felt defeated.

We don't need a miracle against our enemy to fight our enemy. We just need a miracle in our walk to put the enemy on alert. Every day that God helps us is a weapon against the enemy.

Could Rahab have injected her story into Israel's? I have to think this prostitute thought, *If this God of the Israelites can dry up seas for millions of refugees coming out of slavery, maybe God will open up a way for me to get out of this prostitution lifestyle and this godless city.* So she helped the spies and in turn was helped by them. She wasn't just going to survive the upcoming battle; she was going to enter a new future, all because she showed compassion to strangers.

Because of Rahab's kindness and belief that God was with the Israelites, the spies gave her a red rope to hang from the window when the war began. It would be a signal to the attacking army that her house was not to be harmed.

You know how the Jericho war was won? The Israelites marched around the massive walls of Jericho. The walls fell down. The army went in and won the battle.

But here's the crazy part: Rahab's house is on that wall (see Joshua 2:15). Could it be that when the walls of Jericho fell flat, one section remained standing with a red cord dangling from it, announcing to everyone that when you find your people, you find your purpose and your future is blessed?

Rahab and her family were spared because she answered a knock on the door. And when the battle was over, the Israelites got one step closer to the promised land, and Rahab got one step closer to her new future.

GREAT-GREAT-GRANDMOTHER TO A KING

When some of our denominational leaders and I walked into the pornographic theater in Detroit that we were going to turn into a church, the theater's owners turned off the movies and turned on the lights. I watched dozens of men's heads duck down. One person who did not duck down was a twenty-seven-year-old theater prostitute. At the theater, she went by the name Kimutchie. When she went home to her daughter, she was Dianne.

Shockingly, Dianne didn't seem upset when she learned we were taking away her job site. After we launched our church, she came by weekly to talk to me. Dianne had no church background, and the little she knew wasn't particularly accurate. One day, for instance, Dianne asked me to pray for her. As I placed my hand gently on her shoulder, she pulled away. "I'm sorry. Don't pray. I don't have any money," she exclaimed. I was dumbfounded. *What does money have to do with prayer?* She explained that she used to ask other preachers in the community to pray for her, and they would charge her $25 for a prayer and then give her a Bible verse that could serve as her lucky lottery number. That was her understanding of religion.

I opened my Bible to Matthew 7:21 where Jesus said, "Not everyone who says to Me, 'Lord, Lord,' will enter the kingdom of heaven." I told her that just because someone uses the title reverend doesn't mean they are one. Over the course of time, I took this newly enlightened woman on a journey through the Scriptures. When she read through the apostle Paul's letter to the Romans about how to have a changed life, she asked, "Father Tim, are you saying if I give my heart to Jesus, when I die and go to heaven I will live forever? I won't have to cry myself to sleep every night? And I will be a new person?" We turned to the last book of the Bible, and she read out loud these words: "He will wipe away all tears from their eyes, and there shall be no more death, nor sorrow, nor crying, nor pain. All of that has gone forever" (Revelation 21:4 TLB).

She wanted that kind of life. I had the privilege of leading this ex-prostitute to Christ. Dianne discovered that day that there was a Man who would love her unconditionally. He would not strip her bit by bit of her identity, but that Man would come into her life and give her a reason to live. Jesus would redefine her life.

Dianne found a spiritual family at Revival Tabernacle. She turned away from her previous lifestyle and married a deacon from another local church. I'm convinced we bought the theater and started a church so that, when Dianne eventually died of AIDS, she would live forever with Jesus. When we moved in, she found her people, and she found her destiny.

This is part of the process of God. He connects Jericho prostitutes with spies and Detroit prostitutes with pastors so they can be what God has called them to be.

I suspect that if Rahab had stayed in Jericho, she may have died early in life. Instead, after she met the two Israelite spies, she got a new people, a new home, and a new life. And when she went to live with the Israelites, she was lengthening not only her life but her legacy as well. Rahab married a man named Salmon after she left Jericho, and they had a son named Boaz. Boaz married Ruth, and their son was Obed. Obed's son was Jesse. Jesse had multiple sons, one of whom was David—who went on to become king of Israel. That's right—Rahab the prostitute was the great-great-grandmother of King David. We find this information in Matthew 1, the genealogy of Jesus— which means that Rahab was the ancestor not only of King David, but also of Jesus, the King of kings.

Only God can write these kinds of stories over people's lives.

CHAINED TO THE PAST

I have seen prostitutes who have *changed*, but I've seen many others who were *chained*—all because their past wouldn't let them go.

Rahab went on to hold a place in the lineage of Jesus Christ, yet in some ways even she remained chained to her past. Almost every time Rahab's name is mentioned in the Bible, in both the Old and the New Testaments, this phrase follows her: "Rahab, the prostitute." Think about that for a moment. What if every time people said your name, they also would be describing the worst season of your life? Can you imagine having that label connected to your name continually? Every time someone said it, I bet you'd want to scream, "That's not me anymore!"

It's horrible to even think about our name being permanently associated with our worst season.

DAN the thief.
DIANNE the embezzler.
SID the adulterer.
EVELYN the baby aborter.
MAX the wife beater.
JENNIFER the divorcée.
CAMERON the porn addict.
JOSÉ the alcoholic.
BOBBY the unemployed.

Rahab's tagline—Prostitute—was like handcuffs chaining her to her awful past. But her past was not her legacy. Her experience with the two spies demonstrates that when we find our people, we find our purpose. And when we find our purpose, our past is no longer the sole label defining us.

NO FISHING ALLOWED

One night in an inner-city church service, a young woman felt the tug of God on her heart. She responded to His call and accepted Jesus as her Savior and Lord. The young woman's rough past included alcohol and drug abuse, as well as prostitution. But the change in her was clear.

As time went on, she became a faithful member of the church and eventually became involved in teaching young children. Soon this young woman caught the eye and heart of the pastor's son. As the relationship grew, they began to make wedding plans.

And that's when the problems began. About half of the church thought that a woman with her past was unsuitable for a pastor's son. The members began to argue and decided to call a meeting in the sanctuary. The people put forth their arguments, and tensions increased. Things were getting completely out of hand.

The young woman became upset about the things that were being said about her past. When she began to cry, the pastor's son stood to speak. "My fiancée's past is not what is on trial here. What you are questioning is the ability of the blood of Jesus to wash away sin. Today you have put the blood of Jesus on trial. So, does it wash away sin or does it not?"

The whole church began to weep as they realized they had been slandering the blood of the Lord Jesus Christ. They started to realize that if the blood of Jesus does not cleanse another person completely of their sin, then it cannot cleanse *them* completely of their sin either. And if that's the case, then we're *all* in a lot of trouble.[1]

Forgiving others is one of the biggest challenges any of us face. An even greater challenge, though, is forgiving ourselves. Karl Menninger, the noted twentieth-century psychiatrist, once said that if he could convince the patients in his psychiatric hospital that their sins were forgiven, 75 percent of them would be able to walk out the next day.

In one of his best-loved psalms, David declares the freedom and forgiveness God offers us:

> Let all that I am praise the LORD;
>> may I never forget the good things he
>> does for me.
> He forgives all my sins
>> and heals all my diseases.
> He redeems me from death
>> and crowns me with love and tender
>> mercies.
> He fills my life with good things.
>> My youth is renewed like the eagle's!
>> (Psalm 103:2–5 NLT)

Holocaust survivor and preacher Corrie ten Boom said, "When I confessed them [my sins] to the Father, Jesus Christ washed them in His blood. They are now cast into the deepest sea and a sign is put up that says No FISHING ALLOWED."[2] Her words acknowledge a truth that many of us can relate to: we know we are forgiven, and yet we struggle to walk in forgiveness. We keep ourselves chained to our past.

Hebrews 8:12 declares, "For I [the Lord] will be merciful toward their wrongdoings, and their sins I will no longer remember."

When we struggle with the past, we always have to ask ourselves, *Whose memory wins? Mine, others', or God's?* Why do we keep remembering what God says He will remember no more? The voice of our past sin is loud, but the voice of God should and *must* be louder:

"What can wash away my sin, nothing but the blood of Jesus."[3]

When we feel chained to the past, tempted to fish for the sins Jesus washed away, we need people around us to remind us that we are not our past. The two Israelite spies would be those encouragers for Rahab, just as the pastor's son was for his fiancée.

It's not hard to find people who will remind you of what you were, but it takes work to find people who will encourage you to be what God has called you to be. When you find voices that will push you forward into the future, hold them close, for they are unique and rare.

A WINDSHIELD PERSPECTIVE

We all face the temptation to keep looking back instead of walking forward. Keep in mind that the windshield of our car is larger than the rearview mirror. Looking behind us, fixating on the past, can keep us from moving forward into the life that God has planned for us.

The children of Israel, shortly after leaving four hundred years of slavery, found themselves talking too much about the rearview mirror. And then one day, their past crept up on their freedom. They were standing on the banks of the Red Sea. Behind them was their past—the Egyptian army was poised to take them back to their old lives in chains. God's answer to them is found in the front windshield. Listen to what Moses says:

> "Do not fear! Stand by and see the salvation of the LORD, which He will perform for you today; for the Egyptians whom you have seen today, you will never see them again, ever. The LORD will fight for you, while you keep silent."
>
> Then the LORD said to Moses, "Why are you crying out to Me? Tell the sons of Israel to go forward."
> (Exodus 14:13–15)

God interrupts Moses's big speech and says, "Just tell them to stop crying and go forward." That's windshield talk. God was telling them if they walked forward, he was going to take care of their past.

All you have to do is walk. God will divide a Red Sea and help you walk away from your past. You won't need a weapon to fight it—just go forward.

I really believe forward was the answer for Rahab too.

As Rahab looked through the windshield and went forward, her story got even more amazing. She is mentioned in two important passages in the New Testament. When the Bible talks about faith, guess who makes the Hebrews 11 Faith Hall of Fame? Yes, Rahab! Hebrews 11:31 reads, "By faith the prostitute Rahab did not perish along with those who were disobedient, after she had welcomed the spies in peace." Additionally, James uses Rahab—alongside Abraham—to explain the biblical principle of faith and works:

> Was our father Abraham not justified by works when he offered up his son Isaac on the altar? You see that faith was working with his works. . . . You see that a person is justified by works and not by faith alone. In the same way, was Rahab the prostitute not justified by works also when she received the messengers and sent them out by another way? (James 2:21–22, 24–25)

Because she opened her door and believed the Red Sea story, Rahab is listed next to the father of faith, Abraham, so the church can learn that talk is cheap but actions are priceless.

FIND YOUR PEOPLE

How does all this happen to a prostitute in a city that is about to be destroyed? How does an immoral past turn into a key New Testament faith person? How can *you* begin to leave the past behind and start your journey toward an amazing future? The best place to start is to find your people—and the best place to find your people is among the people of God, the church.

I was reading some letters written by Eugene Peterson and was reminded how we have missed the purpose of the church. Some people get so frustrated with the church, finding a reason to leave because of the people "I have nothing in common with," he writes.[4] Here is what you should remember: God has something in common with each person in your church! The church is God's thing, not yours. He does not preselect people who are able to get along with everyone and all enjoy the same things. Why do you think they got saved in the first place? This is the church, for goodness' sake. If you knew the past of the people you're sitting next to, you would quite likely be scared to death. Thank God they are in the church. You don't even want to know what they used to do. If you choose a church based on the people you have things in common with, you want a club, not a church. The church is not a natural community composed of people with common interests; it is a supernatural community.

One of my preacher friends says he can tell someone's

future by reading their palms. Before you judge him, let me tell you what he does. He makes the person hold out their hands, palms up, and touches all five of their fingers and says, "Tell me the top five people in your life, and I'll tell you what your future will look like." That is genius. Five fingers, five key relationships. I have to believe that for a Jericho prostitute, two of her fingers would be two Israelite spies.

Rahab has nothing in common with the two Israelite spies. But she took a chance and opened up a door to her future. I can imagine that she looked like a visitor in a church, carrying all of her belongings in her hands with her family trailing behind her, walking into Israel's base camp wondering, *Will they accept me? They don't look like my Jericho friends.* Rahab did not stop though. She kept walking, and that faith walk took her into her future—a future that turned into an amazing legacy.

Find a church and find your people.

THREE FEET FROM GOLD

There's a story going around that during the California gold rush in the 1800s, two brothers sold all they had and went prospecting for gold in the West. They discovered a vein, staked a claim, and got down to the business of getting the gold ore out of the mine. They dug deep and all went well at first, but then a strange thing happened. The vein of gold ore disappeared! They had come to the end of the rainbow, and the pot of gold was not there.

The brothers continued to pick away, but without much conviction or success. The time finally came for them to give up, so they sold their equipment and their claim rights for a few hundred dollars and took a train back home.

The man who bought the rights hired an engineer to examine the rock strata of the mine. The engineer recommended that he dig in the same spot where the former owners had left off. The new owner started digging and had dug only three feet before he struck gold. Here's the thing: had the two brothers kept digging, they would have been millionaires.

Three feet away from gold.[5]

I wish Cynthia would have dug just a little deeper that morning. I truly believe she would have struck gold. Rahab, the prostitute, will always stand as a story of what happens to us when we open the door to God's people: we strike gold.

DISCUSSION QUESTIONS

1. Do you have a story of meeting someone who changed your future in a good way? Share it with the group.
2. Have everyone in your group do the palm-reading test. Palms out. Count the five fingers and ask everyone to name the five most important relationships to them. One caveat—you can't say spouse, kids, and family.
3. Let's invite someone to church. Someone that you think can use a new future. Let's pray for each person we are going to invite to church this week, believing if they find their people, they will find their future.

CHAPTER 7

SHIFTING FOCUS AND MAKING HISTORY WITH NEHEMIAH

God's getting you ready for what he
already has ready for you.
Joseph Garlington, four-part teaching series

Bartenders always seem to hear other people's stories but never get to tell their own. They listen to someone pour out their soul over their shot glass, and then they offer condolences or encouragement.

In the Bible, we find the story of a bartender who wasn't listening to stories but was writing his own. This bartender was making history that is still remembered today. His name was Nehemiah, and he built a wall when everything in his world said doing so was impossible.

How did this man, whose job was to serve drinks to royalty, become a governor of the most significant city for the Jewish people? How did that bartender design one of the most important structures of that city? God had a story for Nehemiah—a story that demonstrates how this man went from making a living to making history.

WRONG PLACE, WRONG TIME

The prophet Jeremiah told the children of Israel to stop telling a thousand-year-old story. This admonition came just before one of the darkest times in Israel's history—the Babylonian captivity. The Israelites would be taken captive due to their disobedience and made subject to their conquerors for seventy years. Just before Nebuchadnezzar invaded Jerusalem and stole the next generation of people, Jeremiah says these words:

> "Therefore behold, days are coming," declares the Lord, "when it will no longer be said, 'As the Lord lives, who brought up the sons of Israel out of the land of Egypt,' but, 'As the Lord lives, who brought up the sons of Israel from the land of the north.'" (Jeremiah 16:14–15)

For a thousand years, the Israelites had talked about Moses, about how God delivered them from Egypt by ten plagues, and how an entire sea had opened up for them to pass through. It's a powerful story, but even powerful stories can freeze people in the past with no clear direction for the future. Friend and mentor R. T. Kendall put it like this: "Sometimes the greatest opposition to what God wants to do next comes from those who were on the cutting edge of what God did last."[1]

Jeremiah told the Israelites to stop reminiscing about the past because he knew that God was preparing a new story and a new cast of heroes. In the words of George Lucas in the novel *Star Wars: A New Hope*, these heroes "were in the wrong place at the wrong time. Naturally they became heroes."[2] Babylon was the wrong place. Captivity was the wrong time. Get ready for new heroes.

God would raise up a queen who would stop a genocide. Her name was Esther. Three teens would stand while everyone bowed to an idol, and they would miraculously come out of a furnace unburned. They are known to the world as Shadrach, Meshach, and Abednego. Against all odds, Ezra would build a temple against all odds that had been ravaged by an enemy invasion. And a bartender would become governor and build a wall in fifty-two days when it should have taken years.

Jeremiah said new heroes and new stories are coming. And they did come.

PEOPLE WHO "THINK DIFFERENT"

When Steve Jobs, the founder of Apple, died, an old Apple commercial from 1997 resurfaced and went viral on YouTube. The ad attempted to rebrand Apple products when Jobs became in charge. The tagline was "Think different." In the commercial, they showed a collage of photographs and film footage of people who have invented and inspired, created and sacrificed, to improve the world, to make a difference. They showed Bob Dylan, Amelia Earhart, Frank Lloyd Wright, Maria Callas, Muhammad Ali, Martin Luther King Jr., Jim Henson, Albert Einstein, Pablo Picasso, and Mahatma Gandhi. As the images rolled by, a voice read this poem:

> Here's to the crazy ones, the misfits, the rebels, the trouble-makers, the round pegs in the square holes . . . the ones who see things differently—they're not fond of rules. And they have no respect for the status quo. You can quote them, disagree with them, glorify or vilify them, but the only thing you can't do is ignore them because they change things . . . they push the human race forward, and while some may see them as the crazy ones, we see genius, because the ones who are crazy enough to think that they can change the world, are the ones who do.[3]

Nehemiah was one of those "crazy ones." He believed he could help his people change their corner of the world by building a wall to fortify their city. He faced opposition and hardship—but he went down in history as a force of change.

AN INTERESTED LISTENER

The Old Testament books of Ezra, Esther, and Nehemiah dealt with life after the Babylonian exile, when fifty thousand exiles returned from the regions to which they had been scattered to start a new life in Israel. These three books share three massive stories: a temple is rebuilt, a genocide is averted, and a protective wall is erected. New challenges are ahead for the exiles, but God will raise up the right people to meet those challenges.

Ezra took the lead in rebuilding the temple. The project was so massive and faced such severe opposition that the work stopped for sixteen years. People got tired and turned to spending their resources for their own homes instead of the temple. God raised up the prophets Haggai and Zechariah to rebuke and inspire Israel to start building again. And the temple was finished four years later.

As work on the temple neared the end, another story unfolded. A genocidal edict was signed in Persia because a madman wanted to kill every Jew. Only courage and a miracle could stop this murderous spirit. God raised up a hero in the palace, Queen Esther, to save His people.

And then just a few years after that, another story

unfolded. A bartender in Persia heard about the condition of Jerusalem. G. K. Chesterton, English writer and Christian apologist from almost a century ago, said, "There is no such thing on earth as an uninteresting subject; the only thing that can exist is an uninterested person."⁴ Nehemiah became an interested listener, and the story he heard lit a fire in him:

> Now it happened . . . that Hanani, one of my brothers, and some men from Judah came; and I asked them about the Jews who had escaped and had survived the captivity, and about Jerusalem. And they said to me, "The remnant there in the province who survived the captivity are in great distress and disgrace, and the wall of Jerusalem is broken down and its gates have been burned with fire." (Nehemiah 1:1–3)

Hearing his friends describe the city he loved did something to Nehemiah. His reaction drove him to tears and to prayer: "Now when I heard these words, I sat down and wept and mourned for days; and I was fasting and praying before the God of heaven" (Nehemiah 1:4). He was mourning and weeping for a city he had never been to. Nehemiah was born in captivity in Persia. And yet a description of the ruins in Jerusalem overwhelmed a palace bartender, and as a result, history was reshaped.

I've heard it said (though I don't recall who said it), "Don't settle to simply know what God saved you *from* but discover what God saved you *for.*" Nehemiah was about to come to grips with what God saved him for.

DRIVEN TO YOUR KNEES

David Wilkerson was once asked by his grandchildren, "How could God exist and yet there is so much suffering all around?" Listen to one of the greatest apologetic responses I've ever heard on this controversial topic. David replied, "First, the people who complain the most about this question do the least about it. And second, I don't concern myself with this question anymore. I have determined to spend the rest of my life helping everyone who is suffering."[5]

Enter Nehemiah. When Nehemiah learned from his friend Hanani about the suffering of his people, he didn't complain. Instead, he prayed.

Stories are powerful. May we continue to listen to others' stories and even tell our own stories. You never know who is listening and who will rise to be a hero and a wall builder.

One of the key marks of something being birthed in the soul of a future wall builder is seeing tragic stories drive you to your knees. It's one of the first signs that a change may be coming to your life. I have heard tragic stories. I have been outraged, complained, cried, given money, and even gone to the spot of the tragedy. But being driven to prayer means something deeper is happening. Prayer births a burden. And a burden is the precursor to doing something about it.

Nehemiah didn't realize that being driven to his knees would also result in putting down the "cupbearer" title and saying yes to the "wall builder" title.

FROM PRAYER TO SOLUTIONS

Loren Cunningham, the founder of a world missions organization called Youth with a Mission, is listed in the Guinness Book of World Records as the first missionary to travel to every country on the planet. "If you see someone taking responsibility," he once said, "give that person authority. If you see someone looking for authority, watch out!"[6]

Nehemiah took responsibility not only when he prayed but also when God opened a door for him to share his burden with the king of Persia. Nehemiah's concern for his suffering people was so strong that he was willing to risk his life to bring change. Give that man authority!

Nehemiah was one of those people who wore his emotions on his sleeve. One day, when he came into the king's presence, the king said to him, "Why is your face sad, seeing you are not sick? This is nothing but sadness of the heart" (Nehemiah 2:2 ESV). Nehemiah responded in fear. Why? Because in those days, being sad in the presence of the king you were serving drinks to was a no-no. The penalty for displaying emotion was death. Royalty loved living in a fantasy world where everything was okay and the world was wonderful. So when Nehemiah served him with a sad face, he was risking his life. He had a right to feel afraid.

The movement to our destiny will have faith and fear walking together. Courage is not the absence of fear. We can be courageous and fearful at the same time. Another way to put it is courage is fear that has said its prayers. Nehemiah had said his prayers. So when the king asked him what was wrong and Nehemiah found himself at a crossroad between apologizing or speaking with authority, he chose the latter: "And I said to the king, 'May the king live forever. Why should my face not be sad when the city, the site of my fathers' tombs, is desolate and its gates have been consumed by fire?'" (Nehemiah 2:3–4). This man was taking responsibility, and the king seemed to realize it. He asked, "What would you request?" (Nehemiah 2:4).

And now a prayerful man can answer the king's question. He was not an offended man. He was not an angry man. He was a praying man.

What came next is one of my favorite nonverbal parts of Scripture. No words were spoken, but a lot was being said. Nehemiah said, "I prayed to the God of heaven" (Nehemiah 2:4). Nehemiah didn't answer the king's question. Instead, he prayed to the King of Israel. What did Nehemiah pray? Perhaps it was something like, "Lord, give me courage. Tell me what to say. Fill my mouth when I open it." I love that Nehemiah talked to God in that instant before talking to the king. Because when he opened his mouth, "let the games begin"—and destiny starts for Nehemiah. I truly believe one impromptu prayer marked the beginning of his future.

In an interview with Anthony Gell, leadership expert Brian Tracy says, "Leaders think and talk about the solutions; followers think and talk about the problems."[7] Here is what Nehemiah said when he opened his mouth: "I said to the king, 'If it pleases the king, and if your servant has found favor before you, I request that you send me to Judah, to the city of my fathers' tombs, that I may rebuild it" (Nehemiah 2:5).

The burdened man and the praying man had become a solutions man. Nehemiah spoke boldly in the presence of the most powerful man on the planet and said, "Send me home, and I will rebuild the broken walls." Sounds something like Isaiah's words before the King of kings: "Here am I. Send me!" (Isaiah 6:8).

YOU HAVE TO SPEAK UP SO PEOPLE CAN HEAR

The great Baptist pastor Vance Havner challenged us to speak up: "We are so afraid of being offensive that we are not effective."[8] Nehemiah risked it all to speak up.

Nehemiah risked offending the king with his speech and his ask. He was asking the king of the nation that brought Israel into captivity to approve an exodus, to allow people to return to Jerusalem to rebuild a wall of protection around their city. On paper, it doesn't make sense. He was asking his employer to release him from his job as cup-bearer so he could become an architect.

When God grips the heart with a burden, God will also fill our mouths with audacious asks.

Nehemiah was bold. Nehemiah was courageous. And Nehemiah got more than he asked for. He got permission. He got supplies from Persia to build. And Nehemiah got protection from the army. He got it all by simply saying, "Let me go and rebuild the wall."

There comes a time when you must go public with your burden and vision. It's the moment that will catapult you from your job to your calling. When the words come out of your mouth, there is no turning back. Once you go public with what's in your heart, things tend to move at super-sonic speed. When someone speaks to you about tragedy within a nation you've never been to and it drives you to your knees, trust the process. When for some supernatu-ral reason you can't keep your mouth shut and the burden leaks out in an unexpected conversation, trust the process. You just went public. You thought it was a normal day at work, and God made a way.

DISTURB THE PRESENT

On November 8, 2007, Hebrew University archaeologist Eilat Mazar announced the discovery of a thirty-meter section of the wall built by Nehemiah. The wall was unearthed just south of the old city of Jerusalem.[9] A twenty-five-hundred-year-old wall was still there. Nineteenth-century philosopher William James once said, "The great use of a life is to spend it on something that outlasts it."[10] And this was certainly true for Nehemiah. His wall outlasted his life. I've seen it with my own eyes. I was in Israel and saw the remnants of the wall built under the supervision of an ex-bartender in 444 BC.

When most people would have been angry with the Persians or disgusted with the residents of Jerusalem, Nehemiah saw the future. I'm not sure he ever thought of himself as the one whom God would use to repair the wall. But in order for God to use us, we have to expect personal upheaval in our soul and our circumstances, which is what happened to the founders of the Salvation Army, William and Catherine Booth, in 1865.

William Booth had reached a point where he could no longer serve in the conventional pulpit ministry in the church while so many were living in abject poverty in London. Just as Nehemiah was moved to build a broken wall, William's and Catherine's hearts were moved to rebuild the ruins of the lives of the poor in London's East End. Though they faced opposition from the traditional church and its leaders, the Booths persisted in building an evangelical organization to preach the gospel and help the poor. Today, nearly fifteen thousand Salvation Army corps, outposts, and societies exist in 133 countries around the world, engaging in ministry because of the burden of William and Catherine Booth.

Catherine Booth once said, "There is no improving the future, without disturbing the present."[11] The Booths' traditional way of doing church had been disturbed. They went from making a living to making history. So, too, Nehemiah's employment and residence were disturbed. And the bartender became an architect and later the governor.

When we feel a disturbance in our day-to-day schedules, there may be a wall in our future. And then we can pray the prayer of a Christian hero from the past: "Forgive me for being so ordinary while claiming to know such an extraordinary God."[12]

DISCUSSION QUESTIONS

1. Bob Goff said, "Embrace uncertainty. Some of the most beautiful chapters in our lives won't have a title until much later."[13] What is your takeaway after reading this quote?

2. What if God were to say to you as you go to bed, "Tomorrow you'll be able to be paid for your passion"? In the morning when you wake up, answer the question, "What do I want

to be doing?" If the answer is, "Not what I'm doing now," what steps can you take to get there?

3. If you *are* getting paid to pursue your passion, share your story with someone who needs help taking the next step. Encourage someone with your story.

CHAPTER 8

SUBMITTING YOUR WAY TO YOUR DESTINY WITH DAVID

There are many of us that are willing to do great things
for the Lord; but few of us willing to do little things.
D. L. Moody, "To Every Man His Work"

While hoeing his garden one day, Francis of Assisi was asked what he would do if he were suddenly to learn that he would die at sunset. He said, "I would finish hoeing my garden."[1] What an answer! He was confident he was doing what God wanted him to do and living the way God wanted him to live. *Lord, I want to live with such assurance!* Don't we all desire a life with no regrets? Don't we all want to leave nothing undone and do exactly what God wants us to do?

Author Francis Chan quoted these words of Tim

Kizziar, pastor of Sisters Community Church in Oregon—words that haunt me: "Our greatest fear should not be of failure but of succeeding at things in life that don't really matter."[2] I want to get to my destiny and my calling as fast as I can without wasting any time.

Students often ask me how they can find their destiny. How do they know their calling in life? How can they discover what God wants them to do for the rest of their lives? I really do love that question. My answer is always the same. I tell students about a young man who submitted to his father's request, made a cheese delivery, and found his destiny.

Servanthood and submission are two of the best ways to discover our calling. Nineteenth-century American evangelist D. L. Moody reminds us, "There are many of us that are willing to do great things for the Lord, but few of us willing to do little things."[3] The little thing of David—the future king of Israel and the ancestor of Jesus—was taking cheese to the soldiers on the battlefield. On the surface, it looked like a menial task, but it was actually the catalyst, the path, to the great thing. It's part of God's story.

A LESSON IN SUBMISSION

I was just starting my junior year at Wayne State University in Detroit. It was time to declare my major. I had plans to follow in my father's footsteps in law enforcement and the FBI Academy, so I did my undergrad work in corporate finance, knowing it could put me on a path toward Quantico, Virginia, and the academy. Then something happened to me spiritually that complicated my well-scripted path. God called me to full-time ministry in Detroit, Michigan.

Over the past few years, I had been serving at an inner-city church, saying yes to a whole bunch of tasks I wasn't good at. Church leadership asked me to lead evangelism teams each day on the streets of Detroit, sharing the gospel. I said yes, even though I had never done that before. They asked me to play the guitar and serve as the worship leader at the church. I said yes, even though I wasn't a very good musician or singer. Then they asked me to lead a Bible study in a motel where drug dealers, prostitutes, and pimps lived. I was definitely not equipped for that assignment, but I just kept saying yes. I truly believe I found my calling by serving in tasks I would never have signed up for but submitted to.

I just kept saying yes to leadership, not realizing at the time that every yes was a submission to assignments that were preparing me for my future. I felt I was called to preach and pastor, and no one asked me to preach at the church. None of the requests needed the title of "pastor." A friend of mine who was the chaplain for the Oakland Athletics told me he would often say to the players, "The two most important dates in your life are the day you were born and the day you discover *why* you were born."[4]

Discovering what God made you for—that's what happened to me. But none of the tasks I was being asked to do matched the "why." I started to realize as time went on that it wasn't the tasks that would prepare me, but the *submission*. It was God wanting to refine my heart more than my pastoral skills.

STEPHEN THE WAITER

It seems to me that the church's first deacon, Stephen, was born to preach the second-longest sermon in the Bible (found in Acts 7); it would be his first, and last, sermon. Stephen was the first martyr of the early church. His death was the very thing that would prick the conscience of one of the men who became known as the "evangelist to the Gentiles": Saul of Tarsus. We know him as the apostle Paul.

God has a trusted process for His servants. Stephen was tasked with feeding hungry widows who were being overlooked in the church's food distribution program. I wonder if it was hard for Stephen to say yes to serving food. He ultimately submitted to this task, even though it didn't involve a pulpit and a microphone. I truly believe this is God's process.

God will give you tables at which to serve widows before He gives you a stage on which to preach to crowds. What looks to us to be backward might actually be moving us forward.

My hardest submissive yes came from an unexpected source. When I finally told my father that God was leading me to full-time ministry, he rejoiced. And then came his hard ask: "Great, Tim. But you do plan on finishing college and getting your degree, right?" I heard someone once say, "You are not submissive unless you obey joyfully and willingly when you disagree with an instruction from your head."[5] My dad's request was harder than any request made to me by the pastoral staff. I was called to preach, not crunch numbers. Reaching out to drug dealers, prostitutes, and pimps was one thing. But being asked to finish my finance degree when I know God wants me to preach? Now that's too much to ask of me.

Someone once said there are three levels of submission: (1) submitting when you agree, (2) submitting when you don't know if you should or not, and (3) submitting when you disagree.[6] I was at level three. I totally disagreed. I was born to preach. Why would I finish my degree in finance?

I went to the Lord in prayer, assured my answer from my heavenly Father would be along the lines of "We must obey God rather than men" (Acts 5:29). I opened my Bible, hoping to find some verses to support my ambition to drop out of the university in order to preach. I started to look up the word *university* in the Bible. Here's what I found instead: "Children, obey your parents in the Lord, for this is right. Honor your father and mother (which is the first commandment with a promise), so that it may turn out well for you, and that you may live long on the earth" (Ephesians 6:1–3).

Guess who registered for the fall semester? God was going to prepare me for pastoring by submitting to my father. We really can take more ground and advance faster through submission than ambition.

In the life of King David, we find an example of someone whose submission sent him on a journey to greatness. Today, David is forever known as the slingshot kid who killed Goliath the giant. But David entered that battle-defining moment based, not on his slingshot reputation, but by submitting to his father's request that he carry out a menial task.

LEARN TO SAY YES

David went from shepherd to king by submitting. And it all started with a cheese delivery. This is David's story in 1 Samuel 17:17–19:

> Then Jesse said to his son David, "Take now for your brothers an ephah of this roasted grain and these ten loaves, and run to the camp to your brothers. Bring also these ten slices of cheese to the commander of their thousand, and look into the well-being of your brothers and bring back confirmation from them. For Saul and they and all the men of Israel are in the valley of Elah, fighting the Philistines."

If David had thought he was too good to be a cheese delivery man, he would have missed the door that was to get him in front of the king of Israel. Here's what he did instead: "So David got up early in the morning and left the flock with a keeper, and took the supplies and went as Jesse had commanded him" (1 Samuel 17:20). He said yes.

It's a humility test. *Leader* is mentioned fewer than ten times in the Bible. *Servant* (or derivatives, such as *service* and *serve*) is mentioned more than one thousand times. I believe God is trying to tell us something.

Entry ramps into our destiny start with humble, little tasks that typically don't even match what we want to do. Many times, the people who can defeat the giant are never selected because they hate cheese assignments and refuse to accept them. What we define as trivial can actually be massive.

We don't kill Goliaths on "Goliath missions," but on "cheese missions." Don't hate the cheese.

What may seem like a ridiculous request to submit and to serve may in reality be part of God's trusted process to catapult us to our calling.

David's life was marked by submission. The experience wasn't a onetime adventure, but a lifetime habit. When we practice submission to the authority that God puts in our lives, it is a training ground for us as future leaders. We learn to lead better as we submit better. Submission is always hardest under imperfect leadership. It's much easier to submit to people we love and trust, but

God puts leaders in our lives to test our determination to submit.

Saul was a greatly flawed leader, and David was a man after God's own heart. On paper, we would probably think this wouldn't work well, unless the virtue of submission was ingrained in the heart of the godly man. After David was invited to the palace to serve as Saul's armor bearer, jealousy was in the heart of Saul toward David. In 1 Samuel 18, Saul sent David on battle campaigns, with the intention of bringing harm to David because he was a threat to Saul, and yet time and time again, David won the victory on these operations. The lesson is clear: godly character wins over destructive motives and assignments.

If you're working under difficult leadership right now, don't despair. Take a cue from David. David submitted to his father to deliver cheese and to Saul, who had bad intentions—and yet every time David submitted to leadership, he got closer to his calling and became better prepared for leadership. And both of these men were flawed people in David's life.

The world is a better place because people throughout history said yes and submitted to the small, unusual, menial tasks. As author Leonard Sweet pointed out, the world is a better place because Michelangelo didn't say, "I don't do ceilings." The world is a better place because a German monk named Martin Luther didn't say, "I don't do doors." The world is a better place because an Oxford don named John Wesley didn't say, "I don't do fields; I only preach in pulpits."[7]

Open your Bible, and you will see over and over again the story of men and women who had servant hearts, minds, and wills. The world is a better place because:

Moses didn't say, "I don't do deserts."
Noah didn't say, "I don't do boats."
Jeremiah didn't say, "I don't do weeping."
Amos didn't say, "I don't do speeches."
Rahab didn't say, "I don't do hiding spies."
David didn't say, "I don't do cheese."
Mary Magdalene didn't say, "I don't do feet."
Paul didn't say, "I don't do letters."
Jesus didn't say, "I don't do crosses."

Trust the process by submitting and saying yes to serving.

David wasn't led to that battle with Goliath. He was asked to do something small that would open the door to the battlefield. The Spirit did not move him to bring cheese. He went because his dad told him to. As he submitted, doors opened. Acts of service led to him being in the right place at the right time.

If you're in the habit of saying yes to opportunities to serve, here are three recommendations to follow.

SAY YES OFTEN. A youth pastor friend of mine taught me a prayer I use constantly when submission is hard: *Lord, the answer is yes even before you ask.*

Saying yes is easier when we trust the leaders who are asking us to serve. They're the ones who can help us to recognize when God is calling us. I learned that lesson from 1 Samuel 3. Young Samuel, who went on to become a great prophet, was being mentored by Eli the priest. One night, Samuel heard the audible voice of God call his name. God called Samuel three times before Eli the priest realized that the Lord was the one speaking. Eli instructed Samuel to say these words when the Lord called him again: "Speak, Lord, for Your servant is listening" (1 Samuel 3:9).

Every time God said Samuel's name, the boy thought it was Eli calling. I think God's call often comes from the mouths of the people who lead us, such as parents and pastors.

DO EVERY TASK WELL. Be the best cheese delivery boy. Be the best deacon serving widows. Be the best finance student who is called to preach the gospel. I love what Dr. Martin Luther King Jr. said: "If it falls your lot to be a street sweeper, sweep streets like Michelangelo painted pictures, sweep streets like Beethoven composed music . . . sweep streets like Shakespeare wrote poetry. Sweep streets so well that all the hosts of heaven and earth will have to pause and say: Here lived a great street sweeper who swept his job well."[8] The apostle Paul puts it like this: "Whatever you do, work at it with all your heart, as though you were working for the Lord and not for people" (Colossians 3:23 GNT).

Whatever is a big word. *Whatever* is an all-encompassing word. It challenges us to do *every task* as if we are doing it for Jesus.

OBEY EVEN IF YOU CAN'T SUBMIT. Your story may start with reluctant obedience before your heart yields in humble submission. The writer of the epistle to the Hebrews gives a strong admonition in the last chapter of this letter: "Obey your leaders and submit to them—for they keep watch over your souls as those who will give an account—so that they may do this with joy, not groaning; for this would be unhelpful for you" (Hebrews 13:17). What a great challenge to both submit to and obey our leaders.

Though submission and obedience end with the same action, two different attitudes accompany the action. Submission is obeying with the right attitude and right heart. Obedience can have the right action and the wrong heart. Have you heard the story about the little girl who was having one of those "can't stay out of trouble" days? Her mother warned her several times to stop disobeying and finally lost patience and sent her to her time-out chair. After a few minutes, she called out to her mother, "Mommy, I'm sitting down on the outside, but I'm standing up on the inside!"[9] That's obedience but not submission.

The writer of Hebrews teaches that when we get the call to deliver cheese, it's best if we *submit,* but if our heart isn't there and all we have in us is *obey,* we must still do it. Why? Because in the end it will be good for us. Serving and submission get us to the right place at the right time.

Even if we start with obedience, obedience will often turn to submission over time as we see that serving is profitable.

CONCLUSION

The great expository preacher Dr. Martyn Lloyd-Jones once said to R. T. Kendall, "The worst thing that can happen to a man is to succeed before he is ready."[10] To my mind, that person goes into their future with a gift but not with a servant's submissive heart, and they will eventually be a dangerous person.

We live in a culture that promotes gifts but not character. Character is developed in submission and serving. That's God's way, and the end result is extraordinary.

DISCUSSION QUESTIONS

1. As you read about King David, can you remember a cheese delivery you had to make? Share why that experience was important for where you are in life today.

2. Are you ready to say yes to serving in any way that can be helpful? Can you identify someone who could use some help and ask if you can serve them?

3. Have you ever had a flawed supervisor or leader who was difficult to submit to? As you reflect on some of the lessons from David's early life, can you name a few things you could have done better to serve an imperfect leader?

CHAPTER 9

FIXING BROKEN RELATIONSHIPS WITH JACOB

*It's always more rewarding to resolve a
conflict than to dissolve the relationship.*
Rick Warren, Twitter

In the late fifteenth century, the Florentine sculptor Agostino d'Antonio di Duccio began work on a huge block of marble with a goal of producing a spectacular sculpture. After a few attempts to make something out of it, he gave it up as worthless. The block of marble, now badly disfigured, lay idle for forty years. *Forty years!* But then someone else came along—someone who saw hope in the disfigured stone. His name was Michelangelo. He saw beyond the ugly, disfigured block of marble to the magnificent, artistic creation he knew he could achieve with it. And so he began the work of chiseling and cutting and pounding. The final outcome was something called *David*, widely recognized as one of the most outstanding artistic achievements of all time.[1]

Consider these questions as we begin to unfold the insights we hope to gain in this chapter:

- How can we learn to see David in an unfinished block of marble?
- How can we learn to see the best in unfinished things?
- Or, even harder, how can we learn to see the potential in unfinished people?

The Old Testament character Jacob was truly a block of marble, an unfinished work that needed a master's touch. His name in itself was not complimentary. Jacob means "supplanter," a word describing someone who seizes, circumvents, or usurps. Right from the start of Jacob's life, he lived up to his name. Genesis 25:26 reveals that Jacob came out of the womb holding on to his older brother Esau's heel. It was as though he was trying to pull Esau back into the womb so he would be the firstborn instead of Esau.

Jacob came into this world as a block of marble, and the people in his life knew it. In biblical times, people knew that names held meaning. Names were both defining and prophetic. When people spoke the name Jacob, they were already formulating an opinion that he was a rough block of stone. Only God could see in Jacob someone who could be chiseled into a masterpiece.

A TRAIL OF RELATIONAL CARNAGE

Jacob's story starts in Genesis 25 and goes to the end of the book of Genesis. It is a story of relational carnage. Jacob managed to ruin or violate every important relationship in his life. Jacob lied to his dad by pretending he was Esau and convinced him to bestow on him the firstborn blessing meant for his brother. Jacob took advantage of Esau at a vulnerable time and stole his birthright and prayer of blessing. He robbed Esau of the right to lead the next generation. He favored his second wife, Rachel, over his first wife, Leah, leading the sisters to compete for his affection and respect through childbearing. Jacob slept with his wife Rachel's maid, believing that Rachel's desire to have a baby would then be appeased. Jacob lied to his uncle Laban and left secretly with Laban's daughters and grandchildren, offering no warning. If that wasn't enough, Jacob ruined his relationship with his sons by giving one son, Joseph, a coat of many colors—a gift representing his favoritism.

Jacob was one big block of marble. He couldn't get any relationship right. This was an area of his life he needed to fix. But for Jacob to get things right with people, he had to first get things right with God. The apostle John declares how important this order is: "But if we walk in the Light as He Himself is in the Light, we have fellowship with one another, and the blood of Jesus His Son cleanses us from all sin" (1 John 1:7). Healthy fellowship with people is based on a healthy relationship with God.

To walk in the light, we must have a correct view of our sinful self. Walking in that kind of holy light allows us to have healthy fellowship with one another. Because sin always pollutes relationships with selfishness, John ends verse 7 with that hope found in the cleansing blood of Jesus. Walking in the light reveals a lot. But the blood of Jesus cleanses a lot also. We need, as the writer of the old hymn says, "a fountain filled with blood drawn from Immanuel's veins."[2]

Jacob was about to have an encounter with God that would start the process of fixing broken relationships. Jacob was about to walk in the light.

A CHAPTER UNFINISHED

When a couple asked me to perform their marriage ceremony, I told them my typical practice is to give several sessions of premarital counseling before the day of the wedding. They told me, "We don't need premarital counseling. We've both been married several times before." Just because we've done something a few times doesn't mean we did it right. Just because we have experience doesn't mean we have the answers. This couple was like Jacob. They were proficient in ruining relationships and then rushing to start another.

There are people who go from friend to friend, church to church, marriage to marriage, boss to boss, because they can't seem to get along with anyone. They'd rather forge a new relationship than repair the one they're in. Jacob's journey has the potential to help us repair our past relationships. But the patriarch's process toward healthy relationships starts with a wrestling match.

Remember how Jacob swiped Esau's birthright on a lentil soup deal? After being ripped off of the birthright, Esau got so angry that he made a vow to kill Jacob, his twin. But instead of fixing his relationship with his brother, Jacob decided to run to Uncle Laban's house a thousand miles away. Jacob wanted a thousand miles between him and his brother, between his deception and Esau's murderous spirit. Sounds like a good plan for a block of marble. And then, after working for Uncle Laban for two decades, marrying two of Laban's daughters, and fathering multiple children, Jacob decided he'd had enough of that relationship too. Turns out, Laban was almost as ruthless and deceptive as Jacob himself. The story we're examining took place after Jacob had slammed the book shut on the Laban chapter and set off with his family to start a new one.

But we can't close chapters by simply starting another chapter. We can't move forward in life without fixing the problems we've caused in the past. That's not the way God works. Many times, addressing the past is the key to moving into a great future. God will always confront us in our discomfort so we can challenge the Esau past.

God has a process to help us run *into* things when we think we are running away from something else. I learned this lesson early on in pastoring when I jumped to a new chapter without properly closing an old chapter. I brought Elisabeth Elliot, the wife of Christian missionary martyr Jim Elliot, to our city to share her story with Christian leaders. As we walked into the hotel ballroom where she would be speaking, I saw a person from my past whom I'd been avoiding. I'd thought the solution lay in creating a thousand-mile space between us, but God knew otherwise. Here they were, waiting to hear Elisabeth Elliot speak. The Holy Spirit convicted me to make things right, and I'm so thankful I did. The individual was so gracious and so forgiving, and addressing the rift between us allowed me to move on to my next chapter.

Jacob thought time and distance from the Esau relationship would do the trick and allow him to pursue a prosperous future. Twenty years away while working for Laban and a thousand miles between them should have been ample time and space to start his next chapter. Genesis 32 would be a journey, not just away from his old job, but toward God's remedy for Jacob's future. But while Jacob was running from Laban, he was actually running toward Esau.

THERE YOU ARE

After Jacob makes his escape from Uncle Laban, he gets some startling news:

> When the messengers returned to Jacob, they said, "We went to your brother Esau, and now he is coming to meet you, and four hundred men are with him."
>
> In great fear and distress Jacob divided the people who were with him into two groups, and the flocks and herds and camels as well. He thought, "If Esau comes and attacks one group, the group that is left may escape."
>
> Then Jacob prayed, "O God of my father Abraham, God of my father Isaac, LORD, you who said to me, 'Go back to your country and your relatives, and I will make you prosper,' I am unworthy of all the kindness and faithfulness you have shown your servant. I had only my staff when I crossed this Jordan, but now I have become two camps. Save me, I pray, from the hand of my brother Esau, for I am afraid he will come and attack me, and also the mothers with their children. But you have said, 'I will surely make you prosper and will make your descendants like the sand of the sea, which cannot be counted.'"
>
> He spent the night there, and from what he had with him he selected a gift for his brother Esau. (Genesis 32:6–13 NIV)

One of my minister friends once said to me, "Wherever you go, there you are." It sounds shallow and simplistic at first, but it's a profound message Jacob would have benefited from hearing. Places and location don't fix you. Movement doesn't fix you. Only God can fix you.

Jacob thought, *If I can leave Beersheba and leave my relationship with Esau, I will be better.* That did not happen. Then he thought, *If I can leave Paddan-aram and my relationship with my shifty uncle, things are going to get better.* I want to shout to Jacob, "Wherever you go, there you are!" It was *Jacob* who needed to change, not his location.

I have realized over the years that an unhealthy location can still be a God place if our soul is healthy.

Jacob had been in unhealthy places, and he was there with an unhealthy soul. It was time for God to start surgery on Jacob. His surgery would be a wrestling match with God.

WHEN YOU'RE THE PROBLEM

While Jacob was still trying to figure out a way to appease his brother or come up with another escape plan, God was making other plans to turn this marble into a masterpiece. In all of Jacob's planning, he had no idea that the best way to fix his relationship with Esau was to first have a meeting with God. He needed to meet with the One who can chisel and chip away as part of the process of transformation.

When Jacob heard that Esau was approaching, Jacob went right into a "9-1-1 prayer" life. His prayer should have been, "Change me." Instead, he prayed, "Save me, I pray, from the hand of my brother Esau, for I am afraid" (Genesis 32:11 NIV). Jacob was all about personal survival, but he was praying for the wrong deliverance.

Jacob thought he had an Esau problem, but in reality, he had a Jacob problem. His prayer should not have been, "Deliver me from the hand of my brother," but "Deliver me from myself."

Do not confuse your Esau issue with your Jacob problem. Let me explain what that means. We see everyone as our problem. We know everyone else's diagnosis, but we never slow down long enough to get a diagnosis of the state of our own soul. The issue may not be your need for more money, a different job, a different boss, or even a different spouse. It may be something deeper—a different *you*!

Have you heard the joke about a senior citizen driving down the freeway when his wife called him on his cell phone? "Herman, I just heard on the news that there's a car going the wrong way on Interstate 90. Please be careful."

Herman's reply is classic: "It's not just one car. There's hundreds of them!"[3]

Jacob was just like Herman. He thought Esau was on the wrong side of the road, when in reality, Jacob was on the wrong side.

We're all like Herman. Everybody else is wrong except us. The preachers are wrong. The church is wrong. My wife is wrong. My boss is wrong. We need to realize that *we* are the ones driving in the wrong direction, and it's time to turn around and go the other way.

In Genesis 32, Jacob was about to exit the highway, meet God, and get back on the highway, going in the right direction as a new man.

WHAT'S IN A NAME?

In my four decades of ministry, I have counseled people for hundreds of hours. Here's what I've learned: counseling can never take the place of an encounter with God. Every person who needs a breakthrough can't get there until they've had a wrestling match with God. That encounter with God changes the heart so people can hear and obey godly counsel.

Jacob needed to wrestle with God before he could reach the breakthrough he needed in order to mend things with his brother Esau. Until this point, Jacob was a man who was simply playing with religion. He believed in God and when he was in trouble, he prayed to God, but he needed a wrestling match with God.

Here is what happened—the event that changed everything:

Then Jacob was left alone, and a man wrestled with him until daybreak. When the man saw that he had not prevailed against him, he touched the socket of Jacob's hip; and the socket of Jacob's hip was dislocated while he wrestled with him. Then he said, "Let me go, for the dawn is breaking." But he said, "I will not let you go unless you bless me." So he said to him, "What is your name?" And he said, "Jacob." Then he said, "Your name shall no longer be Jacob, but Israel; for you have contended with God and with men, and have prevailed." And Jacob asked him and said, "Please tell me your name." But he said, "Why is it that you ask my name?" And he blessed him there. So Jacob named the place Peniel, for he said, "I have seen God face to face, yet my life has been spared." Now the sun rose upon him just as he crossed over Penuel, and he was limping on his hip. Therefore, to this day the sons of Israel do not eat the tendon of the hip which is on the socket of the hip, because he touched the socket of Jacob's hip in the tendon of the hip. (Genesis 32:24–32)

That night as Jacob met God, it was the first hammer-blow on the path to the marble becoming a masterpiece. The hammer came in the form of a question: "So he said to him, 'What is your name?'" That's a gut punch of a question. On the surface, it may look like pleasantries of two people meeting for the first time. Nothing could be further from the truth.

God didn't ask this question because He didn't know the answer; no, He wanted to see if Jacob knew the answer.

In Genesis 27, Isaac asked the disguised Jacob his name, and Jacob answered, "Esau"—and destroyed his relationship with his brother. Now God asked him, "What is your name?" and this time, Jacob said, "Jacob." He essentially said, "I am a deceiver, a supplanter, a usurper. That is the real me."

It is profound that when Jacob lied about his name, he got another man's blessing. But when he told the truth about his name, Jacob got God's blessing.

A DIFFERENT WALK

That night has gone down in history as "the night Jacob wrestled with God." His loss would actually be a win. That unexpected meeting was the only way to prepare for his encounter with Esau. Jacob not only came clean about himself; after that encounter with God, he walked differently.

When we meet God, we get a new walk. The Bible says that the encounter left Jacob with a limp, a hip issue from the touch of God. In fact, Hebrews 11:21 declares that "Jacob, as he was dying, blessed each of the sons of Joseph, and worshiped, leaning on the top of his staff." He carried the mark of that meeting—a limp that necessitated the use of a cane—all the way to the end of his life. That limp reminded him of a monumental moment.

The most amazing thing that happened after that night

was what God did with Jacob's name. God was unashamed of His new friend. God would forever be known as the God of Abraham, Isaac, *and* Jacob. Regardless of how people knew the old Jacob, it would not deter God from telling the world, "I can be associated with Abraham and his faith. I can be associated with Isaac and his miracle birth. And I can even be associated with a man who screwed up most of his life and most of his important relationships."

No one can deny that it was a miracle that God would attach his name to Jacob. But one encounter with God can heal, fix, and restore what years cannot do. Coming to God is coming into the light of who you are. The story of this man is summed up beautifully in an oft-neglected book of the Bible. Listen to the prophet Hosea tell Jacob's story and then apply it to his readers:

> When he [Jacob] was born, he struggled with his brother; when he became a man, he even fought with God. Yes, he wrestled with the Angel and prevailed. He wept and pleaded for a blessing from him. He met God there at Bethel face-to-face. God spoke to him—the Lord, the God of heaven's armies—Jehovah is his name. Oh, come back to God. (Hosea 12:3–6 TLB)

We don't just get a summation of Jacob's story, but an action step, a challenge for every Jacob out there. The path toward healthy relationships is having a healthy relationship with God.

How did the story end? What happened with Esau and Jacob after Peniel? This is what we learn in Genesis 33.

> Then Jacob raised his eyes and looked, and behold, Esau was coming, and four hundred men with him. So he divided the children among Leah and Rachel, and the two slave women. He put the slave women and their children in front, and Leah and her children next, and Rachel and Joseph last. But he himself passed on ahead of them and bowed down to the ground seven times, until he came near to his brother.
>
> Then Esau ran to meet him and embraced him, and fell on his neck and kissed him, and they wept. (Genesis 33:1–4)

Esau ran, Jacob limped, but they both embraced. God restored a broken relationship between two brothers. The man who ran away from problems was now limping toward them. And that God-given limp made all the difference.

Jacob's story is the story of hope that if someone gives up on your life, God is the Master Sculptor who can change your life. When you come back to God, you get back your broken relationships. Even though your story has a limp in it, *your story is God's story.*

DISCUSSION QUESTIONS

1. Have you ever had a wrestling match with God—a struggle about an untimely death of a loved one, a difficult marriage, or maybe even a hard season at church? Share one or two elements about your Peniel experience.

2. Have you had an experience with God that resulted in something physical or close to it, something similar to Jacob's limp?

3. Would you consider asking for prayer from others regarding a strained relationship and how God might meet and change you?

CHAPTER 10

PRIORITIZING HOME WITH PHILIP

I believe the family was established long before
the Church, and my duty is to my family
first. I am not to neglect my family.

D. L. Moody, *"Thou Foul!" and Eleven Other*
Sermons Never Before Published

When I was growing up, the only Google we knew was the red *World Book Encyclopedia* set in our living room. Our cell phone was called a pay phone, and it was located at most gas stations. The accessibility of information today is extraordinary. Leadership expert Tim Elmore, who wrote a book called *Generation iY*, says that young adults born between 1990 and 2002 represent the "first generation of kids that don't need adults to get information."[1] When we grew up, we needed parents, teachers, professors, and bosses to teach us. Today we don't ask our dad how to change the oil in our car; we go to YouTube, and a stranger shows us how to do it. It's a whole new world.

Another shift that technology has introduced to us is the speed of popularity. Popularity today is synonymous with "going viral." Followers and views are now the words that determine and decide what is in vogue and who is to be admired. Technology not only makes people and things famous fast, but it can also replace them in record time. Entertainers and athletes don't have a long shelf life. Depending on when you read this book, you could be following the music, life, and daily movements of today's phenom Taylor Swift, or you could be asking, "Who is Taylor Swift?"

Fame may be fleeting, but when something is real and authentic, it has longevity. I want to point to someone in the New Testament who went viral because they were real and authentic and therefore had longevity. His name was Philip, and his story began in Acts 6. But it was in Acts 8 where Philip went viral.

THE DEACON WHO ROSE TO FAME

Philip was chosen by the Big Twelve to be one of the first deacons in church history. In Acts 8, Philip went to Samaria in the midst of the Jerusalem persecution and preached. As a result, the city was changed. Here's what we're told in the book of Acts:

> Philip went down to the city of Samaria and began proclaiming the Christ to them. The crowds were paying attention with one mind to what was being said by Philip, as they heard and saw the signs which he was performing. For in the case of many who had unclean spirits, they were coming out of them shouting with a loud voice; and many who had been paralyzed or limped on crutches were healed. So there was much rejoicing in that city. (Acts 8:5–8)

After this stunning introduction, the stories just kept piling up for Philip. In the midst of this Samaria revival, the number one occult leader became a Christian, and Philip discipled him. If that wasn't enough, in the middle of the Samaria church meetings, Philip had a conversation with an angel, who told him to "'get ready and go south to the road that descends from Jerusalem to Gaza.' (This is a desert road.)" (Acts 8:26). Philip left the revival and went to a desert road and talked to an Ethiopian eunuch, who got saved. Historians believe this opened the door for the gospel to spread into Africa.

But Philip wasn't done. For his grand finale, Philip baptized the Ethiopian in a nearby river, with an add-on miracle. Two men went into the water, and only one, the baptized, came out. Acts 8:38–39 reads, "And he [the eunuch] ordered that the chariot stop; and they both went down into the water, Philip as well as the eunuch, and he baptized him. When they came up out of the water, the Spirit of the Lord snatched Philip away; and the eunuch no longer saw him, but went on his way rejoicing." Philip disappeared.

The Ethiopian went on to Ethiopia, but Philip ended up in Azotus (Acts 8:40). That's right—God somehow took this first deacon on a twenty-mile journey instantaneously. Upon finding himself in Azotus, Philip kept on preaching.

Take a bow, Philip; you've achieved fame. Philip is at level 3.

But hold on. Philip may have gone viral, but his fame wasn't fleeting, because Philip was for real. Twenty-eight years later, the deacon who never walked out of the baptismal tank showed up again on the scene.

As we reacquaint ourselves with Philip almost three decades after he rose to fame, what we see is nothing short of proof that if what you have is authentic and real, it lasts. God has a trusted process for His people that gives them longevity. Philip shows us that when the home is a priority, success has longevity. Your story is not fleeting, because it is God's story. And all of God's stories last.

A FAMILY MAN

The great American evangelist D. L. Moody once said, "I believe the family was established long before the Church, and my duty is to my family first. I am not to neglect my family."[2] The psalmist speaks similarly about prioritizing family: "I'm doing the very best I can, and I'm doing it at home, where it counts" (Psalm 101:2 MSG). The psalmist gets it! God always gives a high priority to the home because longevity is connected to our home life.

In Acts 8, we learn that Philip was a strong Christian leader. In Acts 21, we learn that he was a great father too. And it was his prioritizing of family in Acts 21 that makes the stories about him in Acts 8 live on.

The writer of Acts 21:8–9 tells us that Paul and his company "came to Caesarea, and we entered the house of Philip the evangelist . . . and stayed with him. Now this man had four virgin daughters who were prophetesses."

I love that when Paul needed a place to go in Caesarea, they went to Philip's home to reside. They weren't wondering if Philip was some bitter, retired pastor who had gotten burned by the ministry. He was not divorced and living with yet another wife because God had told him to divorce and remarry. It was a home that could provide refuge to Paul and Luke. What a testimony to Philip's integrity.

From this Acts 21 passage, we can focus on three key words to describe Philip's longevity: He had *balance*. He stayed *current*. Finally, he was *intentional*. These are important words as we see God's story unfold in our lives as well.

Let's dig deeper for those who want longevity to be part of their careers and lives. Though Philip's career was ministry, his priorities can be applied to any career. The demands of any job can be taxing. The critical path toward anyone's longevity in any field is knowing how to keep the main thing the main thing. Philip's life and example can help all of us in whatever our career is at present.

FINDING THE BALANCE

Philip took part in a ministry career that even today has dismal longevity statistics. A few years ago, researchers from the Barna Group, Focus on the Family, Fuller Seminary, and the Institute of Church Leadership shared a startling statistic: one thousand pastors were leaving the ministry every month in the United States, which translates to fifty pastors a day. So think of it this way: by the time I finish my day at the church and go home, fifty pastors around the country have submitted their resignation letters.

The research on pastors also showed that more than 50 percent of pastors and leaders are so discouraged that they would leave the ministry if only they had another way to make a living. And 90 percent of leaders who start in ministry end up not retiring as ministers.[3]

So how did Philip do it? How did he last in ministry for twenty-eight years? How did he gain longevity when, even to this day, longevity in ministry seems to be a unicorn?

He found *balance.*

Balance is Philip saying that home life is just as important as church life. It's Philip demonstrating that Acts 21 is just as crucial as Acts 8.

So many in Christian leadership never see past Acts 8. However, Luke and Paul experienced it. (Luke is the author of Acts. When we see the word *we* in the book of Acts, it is Luke speaking of himself and his traveling companion.)

Luke tells us that Philip's home was in Caesarea. Do you know who else had a home in that city? Eleven chapters earlier, we find in Acts 10:1 the other home: "Now there was a man in Caesarea named Cornelius, a centurion of what was called the Italian cohort." Cornelius experienced a vision that resulted in the outpouring of the Holy Spirit just as God carried out in Acts 2, but this time on the Gentiles.

But here's what is significant about Cornelius. When Cornelius needed the gospel preached to him, the Holy Spirit spoke to Peter, who was twenty miles away, and sent him. Why wouldn't God have summoned Philip, who was living in the same city?

My theory is this: Philip was prioritizing home. By fetching Peter instead of knocking on Philip's door, God was showing us that raising a family is just as important as Cornelius's salvation.

This is such an important lesson, no matter what your career is. Proximity to a task doesn't necessarily mean you are the person to complete that task. Keep in mind this principle when faced with a challenge: "Do what only you can do." Only Philip could be there for his children, but a number of other disciples could help Cornelius. Peter was sent to the centurion's house, Philip stayed with his family, and there were wins across the board that day.

THE SEVEN-DAY WORKWEEK

In my early years of ministry, I overheard businessmen imply that preachers only work on Sundays. I knew they were speaking out of ignorance. But after hearing this dig over and over, I'd had enough. "Pastoring a church is much harder than running a company," I snapped at one man. Why? You can be a CEO and have a messed-up marriage, messed-up kids, and a messed-up life, and your job will not be in jeopardy. If you're in ministry, it's different. If your personal life, your marriage, and your children are messed up, your ministry job is in jeopardy. In fact, if only one of these areas is messed up, you're in trouble.

Ministry workers must give oversight to three priority areas of their personal life. They need to take a hard look at their family time, ministry time, and marriage time, and make them priorities.

If you are on a ministry board or serving as an elder, help your ministry worker maintain balance. Pastors can't be successful if they're working six days a week and only taking Saturdays off. Ministry workers need support and permission to be flexible so they can give time and attention to their marriage, their children, and their personal life.

The 1924 Olympic Games were in Paris, France. Canoe racing had been added to the list of international competitions for the very first time. The team favored to win in the four-man canoe race was from the United States. One member of that team was a young man named Bill Havens.

As the time of the games neared, Bill had a dilemma. His wife was pregnant, and she was due to give birth to their first child about the time that Bill would be competing in the Paris Games. In 1924, there were no direct flights from Paris to the United States; the only mode of transportation was a slow-moving, oceangoing passenger ship. Now Bill was in a pickle. Should he go to Paris and not be at his wife's side when their first child was born? Or should he withdraw from the team he had worked and trained with and stay with his family?

Bill's wife insisted that he go to Paris. She knew that competing in the Olympics was the culmination of his lifelong dream. Bill chose the opposite course. He decided to withdraw from the Olympics so he could be with his wife when their first child was born. Being at her side was a higher priority than going to Paris to fulfill a lifelong dream. Talk about putting Acts 21 in front of Acts 8!

The United States four-man canoe team won the gold medal at that Paris Olympics, and as it turned out, Bill's wife was late in giving birth. Bill could have competed in the Paris games after all. A lot of people were saying, "What a shame!" But Bill said he had no regrets. After all, his commitment to his wife was more important than even his dreams.

Martin Luther wrote this in 1522: "God, with all his angels and creatures, is smiling, not because that father is washing diapers, but because he is doing so in Christian faith."[4] And William Tyndale, who translated the Bible into English for the world, reminded us that if our desire is to please God, pouring water, washing dishes, cobbling shoes, and preaching the Word "is all one."[5]

I have just as much responsibility to teach from the kitchen table as I do from the pulpit of our church. I take time to instruct our children and pour into their lives, as I have done for congregations around the world. As my three daughters have gotten to the age of dating young men, I can't simply speak to them from a pulpit on moral purity; they need to hear personally from their father, who prioritizes them and their spiritual well-being. One night, I told my congregation that I had to leave right after the service because I was meeting the high school football player who wanted to take my daughter to homecoming. "I'm going to make sure he's the right guy to escort my daughter," I explained. It was a day for showing the importance of both the Dilena family and the church family. My daughter needed me to make sure this young man was asked the right questions, was given the boundaries, and maybe had a little bit of the fear of God put in him.

Let me finish my Olympics story. There is a sequel to the story of Bill Havens, the almost–Olympian gold medalist. The child eventually born to Bill and his wife was a boy they named Frank. Twenty-eight years later, in 1952,

Bill received a cablegram from Frank sent from Helsinki, Finland, where the 1952 Olympics were being held. The cablegram read, "Dad, I won. I'm bringing home the gold medal you lost while waiting for me to be born." Frank Havens had just won the gold medal for the United States in the canoe-racing event, a medal his father had dreamed of winning but never did. There is something about this story that made Frank's gold medal sweeter than Bill's potential medal. Bill's decision for his home gave him a greater blessing.[6]

STAYING CURRENT

Philip was someone whom God greatly used and continually used. He was the deacon of Acts 6, but in Acts 21 he had become the evangelist and father. He is the picture of a man who was not stuck in the past of what God did, but excited about the present of what God was currently doing.

Many of us have heard our parents talk about how they had to walk to school in raging blizzards, barefoot, up and down hills, against enemy fire. Well, yes, the past *should* be remembered and appreciated, but it's dangerous to talk only in the past tense to our families. When the past is the only story told, it is taken for granted and dismissed. Old stories can inspire the next generation, but I also believe that staying current is the job of every Christian father and mother.

If anyone had stories in the past tense, it was Philip. I can hear him now: "Yeah, I was the first deacon." "You know, Samaria was never the same once I came and preached there. Let me tell you about those sermons." I can imagine that every time Philip saw a water baptism in his church, he was tempted to say, "That's great, but let me tell you about what happened to me when I baptized an Ethiopian." And can you predict how his children would respond? "Yeah, Dad, we know. Two went in, and one came out."

That's why I love that in Acts 21, Philip was referred to as "the evangelist"—a new title that was relevant to where he lived. He wasn't Philip the deacon, Philip the Samaritan revivalist, or Philip the chariot runner; he was Philip the evangelist. He was doing something at that moment that he probably hadn't done before. And so he was armed with new stories to tell of what God was doing.

My wife, Cindy, and I love to tell our children about how God has intervened in our lives and in the lives of our friends. We want them to know the truth of Luke 20:38: "Now He is not the God of the dead, but of the living; for all live to Him."

I have to be careful that I don't continually tell my children, "We took over a triple-X theater in Detroit and turned it into a church." It's a true story, and it's quite amazing. But it happened in 1990. God didn't stop working thirty years ago. So instead I tell them about the people I had the privilege to lead to the Lord this week. I tell them how God provided a miracle of healing for someone I had been praying for.

Let your kids hear what's going on in your lives. Let

them know about God's provisions in the house this week. By doing this, you're teaching your children that God is not a God of the dead, but of the living. Don't lock God in the past.

PARENTING WITH INTENTION

Good stuff doesn't just happen; good stuff comes from hard work. Philip became *intentional* with his home and family. You really can't be a successful parent without intentionality.

A. W. Tozer wrote, "There are those rare Christians whose very presence is an incitement to you to want to be a better Christian."[7] Philip does that for me. He makes me want to be a better father.

I have to believe that Paul and Luke saw the future church in Philip's home when they saw Philip's daughters. Those four girls had to give the apostles hope that the next generation of prophets were well trained. They saw a man who not only served widows in Jerusalem, served a Samaritan city by bringing the gospel to them, and served an Ethiopian on a lone desert road and baptized him, but who also served his family in Caesarea.

There are two standout words about Philip's children that incite me to be a better Christian and a better father. We are told that Philip's four daughters were virgins and prophetesses (Acts 21:9). Those two words breathe *intentionality* from their parents. *Virgin* indicates moral purity. *Prophetess* indicates calling. Virgin and prophetess are not the default programs of youth. Those four girls were dedicated to God and pointed in the right direction. Raising four girls to be virgin prophetesses doesn't happen accidentally. There were good family values behind it. Thank you, Philip, for inciting me.

Danger is on the horizon when leaders know how to serve their churches but not serve in their homes. I believe that God's trusted process in creating longevity in ministry involves prioritizing our children more than we prioritize the congregation we serve. I've told people who have called me with emergency marital counseling needs, "I'm going to support my daughter at her volleyball game right now. We can talk tomorrow." And what's amazing is that they wait. I must first pastor my children effectively before I can lead anyone else.

I can imagine that the apostle Paul may have had Philip's four daughters in mind when he wrote in his first letter to Timothy, "If anyone does not provide for his own, and especially for those of his household, he has denied the faith and is worse than an unbeliever" (1 Timothy 5:8). Philip had a congregation of four, and his whole church was made up of prophetesses. Way to go, Philip!

RAISING PHILIP KIDS

Like Philip, I have four children—one son and three daughters. My wife, Cindy, and I want them to be "Philip kids." We want our children to walk in moral purity and spiritual vitality. Our society will not make this easy. How do we raise morally pure children who know their spiritual calling in today's culture and society? Both purity and calling are under assault today.

In John Dickerson's eye-opening book *The Great Evangelical Recession*, he says that about 70 percent of our children will leave the church after high school. That means that 2.6 million out of the 3.7 million young adults in the church today will leave the faith at some point between the ages of eighteen and twenty-nine. Dickerson then shocks us when he says that out of the 2.6 million who have left, about 35 percent (or nine hundred thousand) will eventually return while the other 1.7 million have left and may never return.[8]

How can we as church leaders preach to and teach everyone else and yet be losing our own children? Our children's future is at stake, and that's why we need fathers like Philip to rise. Our children need parents who live out their faith. The two most effective things we can do are these: be a role model and pray. We must set a good example and be on our knees for them.

MODEL THE FAITH

On one of his college breaks, our son was home with us in New York City. As I walked by the kitchen table, I watched him pause and pray over his breakfast before eating it. Where did he get that? Cindy and I have modeled expressing gratitude for God's provision at every meal.

I challenge every parent to never eat a meal without

pausing to give thanks to God for it. This simple practice instills a spiritual discipline in our children that they take with them into an uncertain future.

PRAY FOR THEM

From the day our children were born, Cindy and I have committed to pray three things over their lives. Our four have heard these prayers every night during our evening devotionals since their early years, and we pray these things over their lives to this very day. It's our attempt to raise Philip kids. It's our fight for their moral purity and their spiritual vitality.

I encourage every parent to pray for these three things:

1. That God will protect their child's virginity.
2. That God will protect their child physically.
3. That God will protect their child's destiny.

If there has ever been a time our children needed to be covered in prayer, it is now.

THE GRAND FINALE

I wonder what we might have thought Philip's grand finale would have been. I'm guessing most people think it was his encounter with the Ethiopian dignitary. Think about it: Philip happened to be at the right place at the right time to share Jesus with this man, and as a result, hundreds of millions of people will come to Christ. What kind of encore could top that? That sounds like an amazing finale to a career in the ministry.

But God knew Philip's career hadn't peaked on that desert road. Philip had a bigger story to tell that the public hadn't yet seen. That bigger story had to do with God's process for longevity, and it would start and finish with the family. It would play out in the lives of Philip's four precious girls.

I can't wait to get to heaven and hear what Philip's daughters accomplished in the early church.

DISCUSSION QUESTIONS

1. Our young people need great role models—those who care deeply about their future. Do you have opportunities to volunteer in your local church's children and youth ministries?

2. For those of you who have children in different phases of life, what three prayers would you pray over them now to raise up your own "Philip kids"?

3. Consider doing something sacrificial for your people, like the Olympian canoe rower did. Can you imagine giving up something important for a greater good?

CHAPTER 11

REGAINING THE ART OF MEANINGFUL CONVERSATIONS WITH JESUS

Man is lost but not abandoned . . . Had men not
been lost no Savior would have been required. Had
they been abandoned no Savior would have come.
A. W. Tozer, *The Set of the Sail*, italics in original

S ome of the Bible's greatest verses capture words spoken
during one-on-one conversations. For example, a night-
time conversation with a frightened religious man gave us
the well-known John 3:16 passage: "God so loved the world,
that He gave His only Son, so that everyone who believes
in Him will not perish, but have eternal life." A conversation with a lawyer who stood up to test Jesus resulted in

the parable of the Good Samaritan. Jesus had one-on-ones with lawyers, rabbis, Roman soldiers, and even an ostracized promiscuous woman at a well.

But what I find extraordinary is that those one-on-one conversations affected more than just the individual. Jesus' conversation with that one woman at the well, for instance, changed an entire city. Conversations have the potential to affect entire families, communities, and nations. Don't ever downplay the potential impact of any conversation you may have on any particular day.

Sadly, we live in a time when one-on-one conversations are becoming less frequent. Technology, though a great blessing, is having a harmful effect on the way people talk to one another. The same technology that helps us reach a lot of people quickly and efficiently also can hinder our ability to carry on healthy conversations.

Technology has taken away our ability to talk with our mouths. Jean Twenge's article in *The Atlantic* asks the question, "Have smartphones destroyed a generation?" She says students are safer today physically, but mentally they are having a health crisis. Smartphones have caused unhappiness and depression in the aftermath of decreasing human contact:

> The number of teens who get together with their friends nearly every day dropped by more than 40 percent from 2000 to 2015; the decline has been especially steep recently. It's not only a matter of fewer kids partying;

fewer kids are spending time simply hanging out. . . . The roller rink, the basketball court, the town pool— they've all been replaced by virtual spaces accessed through apps and the web.

You might expect that teens spend so much time in these new spaces because it makes them happy, but most data suggest that it does not. The Monitoring the Future survey . . . asks teens how happy they are and also how much of their leisure time they spend on various activities, including nonscreen activities such as in-person social interaction and exercise and, in recent years, screen activities such as using social media, texting, and browsing the web. The results could not be clearer: Teens who spend more time than average on screen activities are more likely to be unhappy, and those who spend more time than average on nonscreen activities are more likely to be happy.

There's not a single exception. All screen activities are linked to less happiness, and all nonscreen activities are linked to more happiness. Eighth-graders who spend 10 or more hours a week on social media are 56 percent more likely to say they're unhappy than those who devote less time to social media. Admittedly, 10 hours a week is a lot. But those who spend six to nine hours a week on social media are still 47 percent more likely to say they are unhappy than those who use social media even less. The opposite is true of in-person interactions. Those who spend an above-average amount of time with their friends in person are 20 percent less likely to say they're unhappy than those who hang out for a below-average amount of time.[1]

So many people are thumb- and keyboard-savvy but conversationally awkward. People don't know how to have meaningful conversations anymore.

Thank God that He is not stuck on technology but is involved in people's lives. God knows how to talk to people, even people whom no one wants to talk to. We learn from Jesus on how to be an effective communicator in this conversationally impaired day and age. Indeed, there is no one better at communication than Jesus. His conversation with the Samaritan woman is a fount of wisdom for all of us.

You will want to enroll in Jesus' communication class. By observing and trusting His model for leading a person to a relationship with God, you will see how the hurdles are not insurmountable. Jesus is truly the master communicator, and we will learn so much from just one conversation.

MINISTERING THROUGH EXHAUSTION

The story of the woman at the well begins with a comment about Jesus' physical condition: "He left Judea and went away again to Galilee. And He had to pass through Samaria. So He came to a city of Samaria called Sychar, near the parcel of land that Jacob gave to his son Joseph; and Jacob's well was there. So Jesus, tired from His journey, was just sitting by the well. It was about the sixth hour" (John 4:3–6). Though Jesus was worn out, He still ministered to an unnamed woman.

It has been my experience that quite often God has used me in the most fruitful ways when I was exhausted. If we want to do great things for God, we must learn to minister when we have tired hearts.

It's important to distinguish between being "burned out" and "being tired." Burnout describes not just physical exhaustion; it affects the mind and emotions as well. It's a soul and body that are both running on empty. I can fix weariness with a good night's sleep or a few days off. Burnout is only fixed by stepping away, reassessing, and seeking healing.

Burnout in ministry is not from doing too much work but from doing the wrong work.[2] My friend Winkie Pratney said it this way: "When you get to do what God made you to do, you may get tired in it but never tired of it."[3] I get tired in my job, but I'm never burned out by my job.

Jesus was able to minister when He was tired because He was doing what He had always done—being "about my Father's business" (Luke 2:49 KJV). Jesus' whole life was centered on those words. Jesus never veered from that job assignment. That's why Jesus never burned out on His human side. He was never found doing the wrong work.

He may have been exhausted, but He was never burned out because it was the Father's business to which He was dedicated.

BECOMING NOBLE

We must take note of several important things in the conversation between Jesus and the Samaritan woman. Rather than shaming the woman, Jesus dignified her by speaking to her with respect in public:

> A woman of Samaria came to draw water. Jesus said to her, "Give Me a drink." For His disciples had gone away to the city to buy food. So the Samaritan woman said to Him, "How is it that You, though You are a Jew, are asking me for a drink, though I am a Samaritan woman?" (For Jews do not associate with Samaritans.) Jesus replied to her, "If you knew the gift of God, and who it is who is saying to you, 'Give Me a drink,' you would have asked Him, and He would have given you living water." She said to Him, "Sir, You have no bucket and the well is deep; where then do You get this living water? You are not greater than our father Jacob, are You, who gave us the well and drank of it himself, and his sons and his cattle?" Jesus answered and said to her, "Everyone who drinks of this water will be thirsty again; but whoever drinks of the water that I will give him shall never be

thirsty; but the water that I will give him will become in him a fountain of water springing up to eternal life."

The woman said to Him, "Sir, give me this water so that I will not be thirsty, nor come all the way here to draw water." He said to her, "Go, call your husband and come here." The woman answered and said to Him, "I have no husband." Jesus said to her, "You have correctly said, 'I have no husband'; for you have had five husbands, and the one whom you now have is not your husband; this which you have said is true." The woman said to Him, "Sir, I perceive that You are a prophet." (John 4:7–19)

In his book *The Weight of Glory*, C. S. Lewis writes these potent words about our daily conversations:

It is a serious thing to live in a society of possible gods and goddesses, to remember that the dullest and most uninteresting person you can talk to may one day be a creature which, if you saw it now, you would be strongly tempted to worship, or else a horror and a corruption such as you now meet, if at all, only in a nightmare. There are no ordinary people . . . But it is immortals whom we joke with, work with, marry, snub, and exploit—immortal horrors or everlasting splendours.[4]

There is no such thing as an ordinary person. Lewis reminds us that we have never talked to a mere mortal.

Everyone we talk to will live forever somewhere. That makes even the spontaneous conversations count big-time.

The Jews in Jesus' day didn't think Samaritans could ever become honorable people. They likely viewed the woman Jesus ended up talking to as someone beyond redemption. She was more than a Samaritan; she was an outcast. It was who Jesus was talking to that made this interaction in John 4:7–19 notable.

This conversation never should have happened. The hurdles standing in the way of this interaction were massive. Jesus, a Jewish man, spoke to a Samaritan woman. The prejudices between these two groups were so intense and so fierce that a Jew would never talk to a Samaritan. The Jews considered them to be half-breeds descending from Israelites who had intermarried with Gentiles after the Assyrian captivity of 721 BC. In the minds of faithful Israelites, marriage outside of the people of Israel was anathema.

If that wasn't enough, a man initiating a conversation with a woman and asking her for a drink was outrageous. Jewish men didn't talk to strange women and ask for assistance. And on top of that, a rabbi would rather die than violate these prohibitions. According to the Talmud, there were seven different kinds of Pharisees in Jesus' day— and one was called "the bruised or bleeding Pharisee."[5] To avoid seeing a woman in public, they would cover their eyes and bump into walls and obstacles, thus bruising and wounding themselves. They would rather be injured than see a woman. Jesus crossed the great divide. And thank God He did.

But there was one other huge complication as well. This Samaritan woman was by herself at noon, which told a story in and of itself. Women would come to the town well in groups to draw water for their households, but they'd typically come early in the morning or late in the day to avoid the Middle Eastern sun as they carried the water home. This woman came by herself at noon, in the heat of the day. She was shunned by other women. She was an outcast. She was the talk of the town.

What had she done to earn her town's scorn? Jesus' conversation gives a bit of insight. It seems she was promiscuous. This woman had been with many men. In fact, we know that six men had been part of her life. But this day, this ostracized woman would meet Man #7.

LESSONS FROM A PRO

Man #7 was the greatest conversationalist to walk the planet. Jesus' one-on-one teaches three important things to apply to our everyday conversations, whether with a barista at a coffee shop, a waiter in a restaurant, or a coworker in the cubicle next to us. Let's learn how to talk like Man #7, Jesus. To learn from Jesus is priceless.

FLEXIBILITY

First, notice the *flexibility* of Jesus. Throughout history, He has been known as the "Great Physician." Why? Because He knew what to prescribe for each individual. He did not talk about living water to Nicodemus, and He did not speak about new birth to this woman at the well. He didn't give every person the same talk and the same prescription.

I know what it's like to prescribe the same talk. I once had an encounter with a man in Detroit who asked me for bus fare to get to Pontiac, Michigan. In all honesty, I had been getting frustrated about giving away the little money I had to beggars on the street. But on this night near the Jeffries Projects in downtown Detroit, I'd had enough. I told the man, "I'll give you five dollars, but if you're lying to me, I'm going to pray that God will strike you dead for not telling the truth, just like He did to Ananias and Sapphira in the Bible." I couldn't believe those words came out of my mouth. But the bigger shock was when this gentleman looked at me and said, "I'm lying. Please pray for me." That summer night, I felt like I'd discovered the holy grail that every inner-city minister is looking for. Boy, was I wrong!

The next day, I encountered a man who needed money for gas. He was even holding a gas can. I used the same line: "I'll give you five dollars for gas, but if you're lying to me, may God strike you dead on the steps of the church, like He did to Ananias and Sapphira." I waited for this man to fall under conviction and ask me to pray for him. He just stared at me and said, "I still need the five dollars."

These men needed a physician, not a parrot repeating the same line. They needed Jesus to properly discern each deep need, not some kid using his one-liner. I am so thankful that Jesus is the Great Physician.

The Great Physician is flexible and patient. As He spoke to the nonreligious woman at the well, He didn't just give her Jewish talk, but He used language she could understand. Jesus started with the water talk. But she didn't get it. Notice their interaction:

> Jesus replied to her, "If you knew the gift of God, and who it is who is saying to you, 'Give Me a drink,' you would have asked Him, and He would have given you living water." She said to Him, "Sir, You have no bucket and the well is deep; where then do You get this living water? You are not greater than our father Jacob, are You, who gave us the well and drank of it himself, and his sons and his cattle?" Jesus answered and said to her, "Everyone who drinks of this water will be thirsty again; but whoever drinks of the water that I will give him shall never be thirsty; but the water that I will give him will become in him a fountain of water springing up to eternal life."
>
> The woman said to Him, "Sir, give me this water so that I will not be thirsty, nor come all the way here to draw water." (John 4:10–15)

Jesus was talking about living spiritual water, and this woman was speaking about H_2O. They were miles apart. But instead of Jesus saying, "Listen, do you know who I am? I'm Jesus, and you should get this by now," Jesus simply adjusted His message to make sure it came across clearly.

When our audience doesn't understand us, we shouldn't see them as the problem. We need to take a page out of Jesus' playbook and be flexible enough to adjust our message by using language our audience understands.

So what happened next? Jesus switched from teacher to prophet. His switch was profound. After the woman said, "Give me this water," Jesus took a hard left and said, "Go, call your husband."

Jesus was willing to switch up His communication skills and show His commitment to helping this lost woman understand His life-changing message. He took the Samaritan woman by the hand and walked her into a new life. Is it any surprise that God does the same for us?

Jesus was flexible in His determination to make sure the Samaritan woman got the message. And God the Father was flexible in His communication at the birth of His Son. On that great night when Jesus was born, notice how God spoke. Two different groups—the shepherds and the magi—needed to hear the message but needed a different way of hearing it. How did God accomplish that? To the shepherds He gave angels in Luke 2. And God gave the magi a star in Matthew 2.

Why didn't both groups get stars? Why didn't they

both get angels? Because the message had to be clear, and completely different people were listening. The Jews understood angels because they knew the Scriptures and believed in angels. From the very beginning, in the book of Genesis, angels from heaven have played an important role in Jewish history. And in a field in Judea, an angel came to shepherds to announce the message that God was sending His Son as the Savior of the world.

> In the same region there were some shepherds staying out in the fields and keeping watch over their flock at night. And an angel of the Lord suddenly stood near them, and the glory of the Lord shone around them; and they were terribly frightened. And so the angel said to them, "Do not be afraid; for behold, I bring you good news of great joy which will be for all the people; for today in the city of David there has been born for you a Savior, who is Christ the Lord. And this will be a sign for you: you will find a baby wrapped in cloths and lying in a manger." And suddenly there appeared with the angel a multitude of the heavenly army of angels praising God and saying,

> "Glory to God in the highest,
>   And on earth peace among people with whom
>   He is pleased."

> When the angels had departed from them into heaven, the shepherds began saying to one another,

"Let's go straight to Bethlehem, then, and see this thing that has happened which the Lord has made known to us." (Luke 2:8–15)

The shepherds understood angel talk because they got the message: they went straight to Bethlehem to see the greatest event in human history.

The magi were different. They came from a different nation and a different history. There were magi in Babylon, and Babylonians didn't believe in angels. There were magi in Persia, but their history has no angels in it. But God is flexible. He didn't abandon the magi; He found a way to get His message to where it needed to go.

God didn't get stuck in one mode of communication, saying in effect to these dignitaries, "Either you get it the way I said it or tough luck for you." The Great Physician and the Great Communicator switched from angels to stars, just as Jesus switched from teacher to prophet.

Now after Jesus was born in Bethlehem of Judea in the days of Herod the king, behold, magi from the east arrived in Jerusalem, saying, "Where is He who has been born King of the Jews? For we saw His star in the east and have come to worship Him." . . . After hearing the king, they went on their way; and behold, the star, which they had seen in the east, went on ahead of them until it came to a stop over the place where the Child was to be found. (Matthew 2:1–9)

The next time you see a manger scene during the Christmas season and look carefully at the supporting cast around the baby Jesus, let those shepherds and three magi remind you that God is flexible. Some people need stars, some people need angels, some need a teacher, and some need a prophet, but they all got the message and got to Jesus.

PATIENCE

In the second part of the process of communication, Jesus moved from flexibility to *patience*. Jesus' patience toward this woman was exceptional.

Practicing patience is a challenge. My "Samaritan woman" was my Korean dry cleaner, Hung. I had been sharing the gospel message with Hung for almost fifteen years. Each Monday, I would drop off my suits, and he and I engaged in Bible talk. Hung was religious but not a Christian. He never came to church except to hear the final sermon I preached in Detroit.

Whether he came in appreciation for all of the business I had given him or somehow was hungry for something spiritual, Hung came and listened, and he was born again. I have to believe that every conversation at the counter about who God is and why Jesus died and how to experience the joy of eternal life all added up; it all counted. The patience paid off.

One of the most influential Christians of the twentieth century was C. S. Lewis. Lewis did not take a direct path from his atheistic worldview to Christianity. He went from atheist to theist and then from theist to Christ follower. He believed in God and His existence, but not in Jesus' work on the cross for his sins. Then J. R. R. Tolkien, who had been having regular dry cleaner talks with Lewis, led him to faith in Christ on a midnight walk in Oxford. Patient one-on-one conversations gave us the most important Christian writer in the last hundred years.

Don't miss the important progression of the Samaritan woman's faith. The Samaritan woman described Jesus in five different ways in John 4. First she referred to Jesus as a Jew in verse 9. Then, as they continued talking, she addressed Him as "sir" in verse 11 after the water and well talk. Then the lights suddenly came on. She called Him a prophet in verse 19. But she still wasn't done. She called Him the Messiah in verses 25 and 29. And then, after she told her whole town about her encounter with Jesus, members of her community called Jesus the "Savior of the world" in verse 42.

Thank God that Jesus wasn't sensitive. He didn't turn critical and negative when the Samaritan woman pointed to the racial conflict between Samaritans and Jews at the beginning of their talk. He stayed true to His nature and continued His interaction with her.

Jesus' patience challenges us in our communication process. When we speak, we tend to want everyone to go right to the Savior of the world. We have no patience to move them from sir to prophet or from prophet to messiah.

If we can't get them to call Jesus the Savior, we quickly move on to the next person out of impatience. I believe every conversation we have is meant to move someone one step closer toward the Savior of the world. Patience got Hung, a dry cleaner, to Christ. Patience got an Oxford professor to Christ. And patience for a lost woman resulted in an entire city's turn to belief in Jesus. Stay patient in the process of communication.

FORESIGHT

Finally, as we trust the process, we learn about the *foresight* of Jesus. Foresight is seeing further than the present moment. It's realizing there is more ahead than what is in front of us right now. I have to believe Jesus not only saw an outcast at a well, but also saw a city that could be transformed.

One conversation can shake the earth. That kind of groundswell happened in April 1855, when Ed Kimball, a Sunday school teacher from a Chicago church, saw a teen who attended his Sunday school class at work inside a shoe store in downtown Chicago. Ed waited for his lunch break so he could talk to him about his spiritual life. Though nervous, Ed shared his concern over the young man's soul and eternal destination.

Touched by the sacrifice his teacher had made, the young man gave his life to Christ on that Chicago street corner in front of his place of employment. The teen's name was Dwight, but the world knows him as D. L. Moody, the great nineteenth-century evangelist. One conversation changed Dwight's life.

Did Ed have foresight like Jesus? Did he realize that there was more ahead than met the eye? Whether or not he did, God surely did. The impact of this young man's conversion was amazing. Ed Kimball led Moody to the Lord. Moody's preaching revolutionized Baptist evangelist F. B. Meyer's ministry, and Meyer's preaching impacted John Wilbur Chapman, who went on to become a great evangelist. Chapman met a former professional baseball player named Billy Sunday, who later assumed Chapman's evangelistic ministry after he returned to the pastorate. Through his evangelistic campaigns, Billy Sunday preached to millions of people. In 1924, Sunday held a powerful evangelistic campaign in Charlotte, North Carolina, that led in time to another campaign ten years later. And so on November 1, 1934, at a crusade in Charlotte at which the evangelist Mordecai Ham preached, Ham gave an invitation to receive Christ. A lanky, nearly sixteen-year-old farm boy came to the altar to give his life to Christ. Everyone knew that boy as Billy Frank. The world knows him as Billy Graham.[6]

I think it's fair to say that from the one Ed Kimball conversation in Chicago, hundreds of millions of people around the world have come to know the Lord.[7]

You never know what God can do when you talk to just one person.

Who would have guessed that Jesus' talk with a woman

who had been married five times (and was currently with another man) would change a Samaritan town? John 4:39 reads, "Now from that city many of the Samaritans believed in Him because of the word of the woman who testified, 'He told me all the things that I have done.'" And John goes on to declare, "Many more believed because of His word" (John 4:41).

No one could have imagined that an immoral woman would be instrumental for that city's salvation. It wouldn't be a businessman or the mayor; it would be an outcast. That city, loved by God, found salvation because of this woman who had gone to draw water from a well.

A conversation you have with a father may change a family. A conversation you have with an athlete may change a team. A conversation you have with a single mother may change an apartment building. A true conversion affects everyone in that person's relational circles.

CONCLUSION

While doing extended studies at Oxford University, one weekend I read an article that noted several important statistics compiled by the Pew Research Center. That weekend reading made John 4 come alive, as well as another Bible passage containing another one-on-one conversation. The article dealt with the exponential rate at which Christianity was spreading through the continent of Africa. In 1950,

Africa had nearly thirty-five million Christians. That number went up more than tenfold in 2011, at which time Africa had approximately five hundred million Christians—a number that represented more than a third of its population.[8] Today there are close to seven hundred million Christians on the continent of Africa. Thousands of churches are planted each month to accommodate this explosion of the Christian faith.

How does this connect to a one-on-one conversation? That explosion in that continent is from a one-on-one conversation with Philip and an Ethiopian in Acts 8. I believe the gospel that spread in the Samaritan town (John 4) was the catalyst for other cities in Samaria to experience the life-changing power of salvation. As the apostles in the book of Acts were preaching the gospel, Samaria was still experiencing a touch of God: "Therefore, those who had been scattered went through places preaching the word. Philip went down to the city of Samaria and began proclaiming the Christ to them. The crowds were paying attention with one mind to what was being said by Philip, as they heard and saw the signs which he was performing" (Acts 8:4–6).

In the midst of many people coming to Christ, the Holy Spirit sent Philip away from the crowds and back to a one-on-one conversation—this time with a man in a chariot going back home after visiting Jerusalem. He was an Ethiopian eunuch and a government official: "An angel of the Lord spoke to Philip, saying, 'Get ready and go south to the road that descends from Jerusalem to Gaza.' (This is a desert road.) So he got ready and went; and there was an Ethiopian eunuch, a court official of Candace, queen of the Ethiopians, who was in charge of all her treasure; and he had come to Jerusalem to worship" (Acts 8:26–27). The lives of a multitude of people were still being transformed in Samaria, so it seemed odd to uproot the man whom God was using to impact the crowds and send him to one solitary person on a desert road.

That conversation was going to take some work. Here we have a man running alongside a chariot and overhearing a man reading a Scripture passage and then offering to do some teaching in a one-on-one conversation: "He [the Ethiopian eunuch] was returning and sitting in his chariot, and was reading Isaiah the prophet. Then the Spirit said to Philip, 'Go up and join this chariot.' Philip ran up and heard him reading Isaiah the prophet, and said, 'Do you understand what you are reading?' And he said, 'Well, how could I, unless someone guides me?' And he invited Philip to come up and sit with him" (Acts 8:28–31).

The Ethiopian was reading the book of Isaiah and did not understand chapter 53 and who the prophet was referring to. Then a single conversation took place between these two men that is still yielding results today:

Then Philip opened his mouth, and beginning from this Scripture he preached Jesus to him. As they went along the road they came to some water; and the eunuch said, "Look! Water! What prevents me from being baptized?" And he ordered that the chariot stop; and they both went down into the water, Philip as well as the eunuch, and he baptized him. (Acts 8:35–38)

A Jew had a conversation with a lost Samaritan woman, and a city was changed. And now a Jew talked to an Ethiopian, and a continent was changed. Who would have thought one conversation in AD 31 would have lasting effects in the twenty-first century? The *flexibility* of Philip obediently leaving Samaria for one person was commendable. The *patience* of Philip in gently explaining the Isaiah passage and revealing that Jesus gave His life for sinners was remarkable. And who knows, maybe Philip did have the *foresight* to see that an Ethiopian dignitary who was saved and baptized could help bring the gospel to his country. But there was much more in that one conversation, as well as in the description of what happened to Philip after this conversation. And that's a topic for the epilogue.

DISCUSSION QUESTIONS

1. Who is one person you see each day with whom you'd like to start the journey of sharing the gospel? Ask your friends to encourage you and pray for you, that you will find an opportunity to talk to them and confidently use the process of sharing Jesus.

2. Have you ever known or heard about a person's conversion, which then had a ripple effect in which an entire family was saved?

3. Have you had some great gospel conversation starters with strangers? What are some ways you can go past small talk to do a deep dive into spiritual matters?

EPILOGUE

THE STORY ISN'T OVER

*I never saw a useful Christian who
was not a student of the Bible.*
D. L. Moody

We're not done quite yet! This is an epilogue you must read. Sometimes an epilogue is the section in the book where unanswered questions are resolved—and this is that kind of epilogue.

MINING FOR GOLD

For me, Romans 15:4 is one of the threads that tie all of these stories together. Listen to what Paul reminds the Christian church: "Everything that was written in the past was written to teach us, so that through the endurance taught in the

Scriptures and the encouragement they provide we might have hope" (NIV).

The "everything that was written in the past" includes the stories you just read. Paul was saying these are not just stories; these are *your* stories. They were written for you. When you read a Bible narrative, let it read you. Let the story bring definition to your own story and the details of your own life.

It's important to note that not every story in the Bible ends with "they lived happily ever after." I love that because, of course, that is reality. So when we read someone else's story, it may be more of a warning than an instruction, telling us to not let their story be our story.

We don't have to experience something to gain wisdom and understanding. People often say that experience is the best teacher, but this isn't necessarily true. For example, if it were true, we could spiral into this kind of thinking: *I need to do drugs to know not to do drugs.* John Maxwell wrote in one of his blog posts, "Experience is not the best teacher; *evaluated* experience is the best teacher."[1] And the teaching can come even through evaluating what *others* have gone through. I have counseled people through some of their darkest times and had my mind wander when I heard how they got themselves in a bad place—whether adultery, addiction, or deceit, I would be reminded by the Holy Spirit, *Learn from this. Stay humble. You could be on the other side of the desk.* That was the exclamation point. Always remember that it could easily be you confessing your sins.

R. C. Sproul gets to the heart of why these Bible narratives have not yet inspired us: "Here then, is the real problem of our negligence. We fail in our duty to study God's Word not so much because it is difficult to understand, not so much because it is dull and boring, but because it is work. Our problem is not a lack of intelligence or a lack of passion. Our problem is that we are lazy."[2]

Your Life Is God's Story is meant to help you in the hard work of delving into God's Word for guidance and inspiration. *Your Life Is God's Story* will help you mine for the gold in these narratives. This book is meant to be a tool—not an exhaustive one but an inspirational one to help you get the gold from the other dozens of stories in the Bible. I believe it will be important for you to read these Bible stories straight through. Underline verses, take notes, and then apply the teachings of *Your Life Is God's Story* into the mix. And share with someone else the lessons you learned, which you can do in a small-group setting or one-on-one over a cup of coffee.

The great Baptist preacher Vance Havner was right when he said, "If you see a Bible that is falling apart, it probably belongs to someone who isn't."[3] An unread Bible is like a check never cashed, a meal never eaten, a gift never opened, a map never referred to. When you open your Bible, you are cashing the check, scraping your plate clean, opening the gift, checking the map—and the reward is amazing.

Paul says that one of those rewards is endurance.

I believe endurance comes from a deep place. Romans 15:4 says we learn endurance from the stories we hear. Endurance is a vital ingredient in a race. The Christian life is not a sprint; it's a marathon. So we have to pace ourselves. Some days it's a walk; some days it's a limp; other days it's a sprint. When I see a Christian always sprinting, I know someone is going to be in trouble real soon. The goal is not to go fast but to go forward. The word *endurance* describes the ability to remain active for a long period of time, as well as the ability to resist, withstand, and recover from trauma, wounds, and fatigue. To endure is to put up with, to stand despite encountering circumstances that should make us buckle and fall. Paul tells us that Bible stories can and will teach us endurance and provide us with encouragement. I believe that, in a way, they represent the cheerer on the side of the road during a marathon with the paper Dixie cup containing the water that refreshes you and gives you hope on the uphill-climb days. I'm so thankful God put stories in the Bible, and not just directives. When I watch as others cross the finish line, I'm filled with hope that I can cross it too.

ACKNOWLEDGMENTS

No book is ever the product of the hands of one author only. Dozens of hands all have their unique fingerprints on any project, and this book is no exception. Those hands typed out research, sent notes to encourage, picked up the phone to offer guidance, and clasped together to pray. It's important to acknowledge the hands that made this book possible.

I am grateful to my wife, Cindy, whose encouragement is vital in my life. I always hear her voice to "press on; you can do this." To my assistant, Amy, who tirelessly helped with research and edits—you are a joy to work with. To Dale Williams—you became both a friend and a guide to help me navigate new territory. The counsel of Dr. O. S. Hawkins from the very beginning and throughout the process was invaluable. I'm so thankful I have the privilege to reap the wisdom born out of his decades of ministry.

And finally to my Times Square Church family, who prays for me every day—I could never underestimate the power of prayer.

Your prayers supplied strength when I was growing weary. Your prayers gave me wisdom when I couldn't see the next step. Your prayers provided freshness when my tired soul felt like it was close to flatlining. I love you, TSC.

NOTES

PROLOGUE: FOUR WORDS THAT CHANGED MY LIFE

1. For David Wilkerson's full story, see Gary Wilkerson, *David Wilkerson: The Cross, the Switchblade, and the Man Who Believed* (Grand Rapids: Zondervan, 2014).
2. For Nicky Cruz's full story, see Nicky Cruz, *Run Baby Run: Life-Changing Testimony of a New York Gang Leader* (Newberry, FL: Bridge Logos, 1968).
3. Philip Yancey, *Finding God in Unexpected Places* (Ann Arbor, MI: Vine, 1997), 178.

CHAPTER 1: SHARING SCAR STORIES WITH HEZEKIAH

1. See Kevin Ramsby, *A Fight to Forgive: How to Turn Their Wrongs and Your Hurts into God's Greater Purposes* (Servus, 2016).
2. See Levi Avtzon, "The Tragic History of Molech Child Sacrifice," Chabad.org, www.chabad.org/parshah/article_cdo/aid/4372130/jewish/The-Tragic-History-of-Molech-Child-Sacrifice.htm, accessed August 1, 2023.

3. Michael Apted, dir., *The Chronicles of Narnia: The Voyage of the Dawn Treader* (Los Angeles: 20th Century Studios, 2010). Note: the line appears in the movie but is not found in C. S. Lewis's book of the same title.

4. Augustine, *Confessions*, trans. R. S. Pine-Coffin (New York: Penguin, 1961), 146–47.

CHAPTER 2: TRAINING FOR GREATNESS WITH JOSEPH

1. Quoted in Salma Sultana, "You Can't Have a Relationship without Any Fights, but You Can Make Your Relationship Worth the Fight," Momspresso, November 28, 2019, www.momspresso.com/parenting /food-blogger/article/you-can-t-have-a-relationship -without-any-fightsbut-you-can-make-your-relationship -worth-the-fight.

2. Tom Shadyac, dir., *Bruce Almighty* (New York: Universal Studios; Burbank, CA: Walt Disney Studios, 2003).

3. Teresa of Ávila, *The Life of Saint Teresa of Ávila by Herself*, trans. J. M. Cohen (London: Penguin, 1988), 191.

4. Ravi Zacharias, *The Grand Weaver: How God Shapes Us through the Events of Our Lives* (Grand Rapids: Zondervan, 2007), 60.

5. Winkie Pratney, "Hurt and Bitterness," YouTube, December 20, 2020, www.youtube.com/watch?v=naY GwNv0kHs.

6. A. W. Tozer, *The Root of the Righteous* (Chicago: Moody, 1955), 165.

7. William Secker, *The Nonsuch Professor in His Meridian*

Splendour: Or, The Singular Actions of Sanctified Christians (Oxford, UK: Pembrey, 1877), 27–28.

8. C. S. Lewis, *The Four Loves* (1960; repr., New York: Harvest, 1991), 121.

9. Augustine, *Confessions*, trans. R. S. Pine-Coffin (New York: Penguin, 1961).

10. Quoted in Amy Newmark and Deborah Norville, *Chicken Soup for the Soul: Think Possible* (Cos Cob, CT: Chicken Soup for the Soul Publishing, 2015), 357.

11. R. T. Kendall, *Pure Joy: Receiving God's Gift of Gladness in Every Trial* (Lake Mary, FL: Charisma House, 2015), 48.

CHAPTER 3: NAVIGATING BLANK SPACES WITH ABRAHAM

1. See C. Hope Flinchbaugh, "Why the Revival Flame Still Burns Bright in China," *Charisma*, March 31, 2002, https://charismamag.com/propheticrevival/revival/a-flame-burns-in-china.

2. Howard Taylor and Geraldine Taylor, *Hudson Taylor in Early Years: The Growth of a Soul* (Philadelphia: China Inland Mission, 1912), 387–88.

3. Quoted in A. J. Broomhall, *Hudson Taylor and China's Open Century*, book 4 (London: Hodder & Stoughton and Overseas Missionary Fellowship, 1984), 154.

4. See Matthew Kratz, "Would You Consider Abortion . . .," Sermon Central, July 20, 2008, www.sermoncentral.com/sermon-illustrations/67966/would-you-consider-abortion-by-matthew-kratz.

5. Ronald Reagan, as quoted in Sreechinth C, *Ronald Reagan's Legacy of Word: 1000+ Quotes of Ronald Reagan* (Kerala, India: UB Tech, 2018), 45.

6. Quoted in Harold Isbell, *Every Life Is a Story That Deserves to Be Told: True Stories about Life's Ups and Downs* (Bloomington, IN: Xlibris, 2012), 127. This saying is often misattributed to C. S. Lewis.

7. Quoted in Craig Brian Larson, ed., *750 Engaging Illustrations for Preachers, Teachers, and Writers* (Grand Rapids: Baker, 2007), 472.

8. Adapted from David Mikkelson, "Did Abraham Lincoln Endure Failure before Presidency?," Snopes, August 4, 2022, www.snopes.com/fact-check/abraham -lincoln-failure. This article responds to Roger Knapp, "Lincoln Never Quits," www.rogerknapp.com/inspire /lincoln.htm.

CHAPTER 4: MAKING THE MOST OF OUR WORST DAYS WITH PETER

1. C. S. Lewis, *On Stories and Other Essays on Literature* (1966; repr., New York: Harcourt Brace, 1982), 14.

2. Judith Viorst, *Alexander and the Terrible, Horrible, No Good, Very Bad Day* (New York: Aladdin, 1972), 1, 3.

3. Brennan Manning, *The Furious Longing of God* (Colorado Springs: Cook, 2009), 35, 75, 77, 124–25.

4. Brennan Manning, *A Glimpse of Jesus: The Stranger to Self-Hatred* (San Francisco: HarperSanFrancisco, 2003), 33.

5. See Dan Dailey, "Broken Bulb," Wandervogel Diary, September 8, 2015, https://wandervogeldiary.word press.com/2015/09/08/broken-bulb; see also "Edison: Boy Drops the First Light Bulb," *Family Times*, www .family-times.net/illustration/Second-Chance/200780, accessed August 1, 2023.

6. Quoted in Maryn Liles, "115 of Abraham Lincoln's Most Memorable Quotes in Honor of President's Day," *Parade*, February 20, 2023, https://parade.com/989260 /marynliles/abraham-lincoln-quotes.

7. Quoted in Joel Osteen, Twitter post, June 20, 2017, 8:30 p.m., https://twitter.com/JoelOsteen/status/877 322763442069506.

8. Oswald Chambers, *My Utmost for His Highest: Classic Edition* (Grand Rapids: Discovery House, 2017), December 31.

9. John Burnaby, ed., *Augustine: Later Works* (Philadelphia: Westminster, 1960), 206, para. 16.

CHAPTER 5: APPRECIATING COMMUNITY WITH PAUL

1. John Wooden and Don Yaeger, *A Game Plan for Life: The Power of Mentoring* (New York: Bloomsbury, 2009), 16.

2. Quoted in Michael S. Josephson and Wes Hanson, eds., *The Power of Character: Prominent Americans Talk about Life, Family, Work, Values, and More* (Bloomington, IN: Unlimited, 2004), 83.

3. C. S. Lewis, "Hamlet: The Prince or the Poem?," *Proceedings of the British Academy* 28 (1942): 10–11.

4. Shared by Donnie Moore, personal communication.

5. Ridley Scott, dir., *Gladiator* (Universal City, CA: DreamWorks Pictures, 2000), www.imdb.com/title /tt0172495/characters/nm0000128.

CHAPTER 6: FINDING YOUR PEOPLE AND PURPOSE WITH RAHAB

1. See Vernon Price, "Nothing but the Blood," Sermon Central, April 10, 2012, www.sermoncentral.com /sermon-illustrations/81207/nothing-but-the-blood-by -vernon-price.

2. Corrie ten Boom, *Tramp for the Lord* (Fort Washington, PA: CLC, 2011), 116.

3. Robert Lowry, "Nothing but the Blood of Jesus" (1876), public domain.

4. Eric E. Peterson and Eugene H. Peterson, *Letters to a Young Pastor: Timothy Conversations between Father and Son* (Colorado Springs: NavPress, 2020), 4.

5. Story told in Brian Cavanaugh, *More Sower's Seeds: Second Planting* (Mahwah, NJ: Paulist, 1992), 82–83.

CHAPTER 7: SHIFTING FOCUS AND MAKING HISTORY WITH NEHEMIAH

1. R. T. Kendall, *The Anointing: Yesterday, Today and Tomorrow* (Lake Mary, FL: Charisma House, 2003), 133.

2. George Lucas, *Star Wars: A New Hope* (New York: Ballantine, 1986), 2.

3. "The Iconic Think Different Apple Commercial

Narrated by Steve Jobs," FS, https://fs.blog/steve-jobs
-crazy-ones, accessed August 1, 2023.

4. G. K. Chesterton, "On Mr. Rudyard Kipling and
Making the World Small," in *The Collected Works
of G. K. Chesterton*, vol. 1, ed. David Dooley (San
Francisco: Ignatius, 1986), 54.

5. Shared by Gary Wilkerson, personal communication.

6. "Top 16 Loren Cunningham Quotes of All Time,"
Quotes.pub, https://quotes.pub/loren-cunningham
-quotes#google_vignette, accessed August 1, 2023.

7. "117 Leadership Quotes for Inspiration," Brian Tracy
International, www.briantracy.com/blog/leadership
-success/leadership-quotes-for-inspiration, accessed
August 1, 2023.

8. Quoted in "How to Handle Fear: Part 4," Precept
Austin, January 2, 2020, www.preceptaustin.org/how
_to_handle_fear_4.

9. See Christopher Eames, "Discovered: Nehemiah's
Wall," Armstrong Institute of Biblical Archaeology,
October 31, 2019, https://armstronginstitute.org/204
-discovered-nehemiahs-wall.

10. Quoted in Ralph Barton Perry, *The Thought and
Character of William James* (New York: Harper & Row,
1965), 237.

11. Catherine Booth, *Aggressive Christianity: Practical
Sermons* (Philadelphia: National Publishing
Association for the Promotion of Holiness, 1883), 57.

12. Quoted in Dargan Thompson, "Jim Elliot Quotes That

Will Change the Way You Think about Sacrifice,"
Relevant, January 8, 2016, https://relevantmagazine
.com/god/jim-elliot-quotes-will-change-way-you-think
-about-sacrifice.

13. Bob Goff, *Live in Grace, Walk in Love: A 365-Day Journey*
(Nashville: Nelson, 2019), 255.

CHAPTER 8: SUBMITTING YOUR WAY TO YOUR DESTINY WITH DAVID

1. Quoted in George Sweeting, *Who Said That? More Than 2,500 Usable Quotes and Illustrations* (Chicago: Moody, 1995), 155.

2. Quoted in Francis Chan, *Crazy Love: Overwhelmed by a Relentless God* (Colorado Springs: Cook, 2008), 92.

3. M. Laird Simons, ed., *Holding the Fort: Comprising Sermons and Addresses at the Great Revival Meetings Conducted by Moody and Sankey* (Philadelphia: Porter & Coates, 1877), 45.

4. Shared by Donnie Moore, personal communication.

5. Coty Pinckney, "Submission and Disagreement," Desiring God Community Church, July 19, 2008, www .desiringgodchurch.org/web/2008/07/19/submission -and-disagreement.

6. Shared by Jacob Aranza, personal communication.

7. See Leonard Sweet, "I Don't Do . . .," *Leadership Journal* 15 (Spring 1994: Worship), www.christianitytoday.com /pastors/1994/spring/412032.html.

8. Quoted in "Martin Luther King Jr.: What Is Your Life's

Blueprint?," (speech given at Barratt Junior High in Philadelphia, October 26, 1967), *Seattle Times*, https://projects.seattletimes.com/mlk/words-blueprint.html, accessed August 1, 2023.

9. Cited in Randy Frazee, *The Heart of the Story: Discover Your Life within the Grand Epic of God's Story* (Grand Rapids: Zondervan, 2017), 74.

10. Quoted in R. T. Kendall, *In Pursuit of His Wisdom: How to Get God's Opinion on Any Matter* (Lake Mary, FL: Charisma House, 2015), 86.

CHAPTER 9: FIXING BROKEN RELATIONSHIPS WITH JACOB

1. See Editors of *Encyclopaedia Britannica*, "How a Rejected Block of Marble Became the World's Most Famous Statue," *Encyclopaedia Britannica*, www.britannica.com/story/how-a-rejected-block-of-marble-became-the-worlds-most-famous-statue, accessed August 1, 2023.

2. William Cowper, "There Is a Fountain Filled with Blood" (1772), public domain.

3. "An Old Man Gets an Urgent Phone Call from His Wife While Driving Home," Sunny Skyz, December 1, 2015, www.sunnyskyz.com/funny-jokes/154/An-Old-Man-Gets-An-Urgent-Phone-Call-From-His-Wife-While-Driving-Home.

CHAPTER 10: PRIORITIZING HOME WITH PHILIP

1. Tim Elmore, "Generation iY: Equipping the Future Leaders of Christian Nonprofits," Christian Leadership

Alliance, https://ym.christianleadershipalliance.org /page/GenerationiY, accessed October 6, 2023.

2. Dwight L. Moody, *"Thou Foul!" and Eleven Other Sermons Never Before Published* (New York: Christian Herald, 1911), 65.

3. Cited in Lance Witt, *Replenish: Leading from a Healthy Soul* (Grand Rapids: Baker, 2011), 17–18.

4. Martin Luther, "The Estate of Marriage," trans. Walther I. Brandt (1522), www.1215.org/lawnotes/misc /marriage/martin-luther-estate-of-marriage.pdf.

5. Cited in Os Guinness, *The Call: Finding and Fulfilling God's Purpose for Your Life* (Nashville: W, 1998), 65.

6. The story of Bill Havens I've reproduced here is told in Steve Goodier, "No Regrets," Inspire21, May 20, 2020, https://inspire21.com/no-regrets.

7. A. W. Tozer, *Experiencing the Presence of God: Teachings from the Book of Hebrews* (Grand Rapids: Baker, 2014), 170.

8. John S. Dickerson, *The Great Evangelical Recession: 6 Factors That Will Crash the American Church . . . and How to Prepare* (Grand Rapids: Baker, 2013), 240–41.

CHAPTER 11: REGAINING THE ART OF MEANINGFUL CONVERSATIONS WITH JESUS

1. Jean M. Twenge, "Have Smartphones Destroyed a Generation?" *The Atlantic*, September 2017, www.the atlantic.com/magazine/archive/2017/09/has-the-smart phone-destroyed-a-generation/534198.

2. See Malcolm Smith, *Spiritual Burnout: When Doing All You Can Isn't Enough* (New York: Albury, 1996).

3. Shared by Winkie Pratney, personal communication.

4. C. S. Lewis, *The Weight of Glory* (1949; repr., Grand Rapids: Eerdmans, 2001), 14–15.

5. William Barclay, *The Gospel of Matthew,* vol. 2 (Philadelphia: Westminster, 1957), 313.

6. See Laura Bailey, "The Night Billy Graham Was Born Again," Billy Graham Evangelistic Association, November 6, 2017, https://billygraham.org/story/the -night-billy-graham-was-born-again.

7. See Arthur G. McPhee, *Friendship Evangelism: The Caring Way to Share Your Faith* (Grand Rapids: Zondervan, 1978), 131–33.

8. See "Global Christianity: A Report on the Size and Distribution of the World's Christian Population," Pew Research Center, December 19, 2011, www.pew research.org/religion/2011/12/19/global-christianity -regions.

EPILOGUE: THE STORY ISN'T OVER

1. John C. Maxwell, "Borrowing Experience," *John Maxwell* (blog), October 6, 2011, www.johnmaxwell.com /blog/borrowing-experience, italics added.

2. R. C. Sproul, *Knowing Scripture* (Downers Grove, IL: InterVarsity, 1977), 17.

3. Vance Havner, *All the Days* (Old Tappan, NJ: Revell, 1976), 160.